when you buy this book

EugenR Lowy

Special thanks to Professor Haim Omer, my friend, whose support from the very beginning of creation of this book was essential.

ISBN-13: 978-8026042075 (WORLD ECONOMY)
Edited and corrected to proper English, Anna Bryson

*What happens to the **WORLD ECONOMY** when you buy this book*

Content;

If you asked me to tell you in one sentence what economics is all about, I would probably say: "Economics is a tool that helps allocate and utilize every limited resource available in order to maximize benefits and utility for the community and the individual".

Are you already yawning or frowning? Well, let's try again. **"Economics is the science of a short blanket in a cold room: if you cover your feet your shoulders will be cold and if you cover your shoulders your feet will be cold".**

1. Which comes first, the chicken or the egg? (An Introduction to Money and Product)

Right at the start let me declare my intention to explain the basic mechanism of the world economy, in the simplest way possible and without using a single graph or mathematical equation.

To begin with, the very first and most important economic question is like the well-known riddle, "Which comes first, the chicken or the egg?". Except my question will be, "Which comes first, the Money or the Product?"

Well, for the riddle of "the chicken and the egg" there is no real answer, and same is true of Money and Product, for the one always presupposes the other. At end of the day Money and Product are two sides of the same coin and therefore have no existence without each other.

In the book Product means anything that has any economic value expressed in the form of Money. By the way, this means that services like a haircut are just as much Product as a loaf of bread. Product is always an item exchangeable between purchaser and the seller with MONEY as means used to make the exchange. In the modern economy the only way to sell or purchase products is to take or give money for them. In the distant past, the system of direct exchange of products known as barter was common. How the value of a product is measured in a barter system is an interesting question, but I shall not go into it here, since no significant economic activity takes place in the modern economy without money as far as I know.

Some people worship money and others claim the world would be better off without it, but no - one can actually do without it or be indifferent to it, for everyone has to use it as an instrument for purchasing and selling products. Product comes in a variety of forms, and so too does Money. Just because Money can take different forms, people sometimes think of it as having some of the qualities of Product. As we shall see, functionally Money can sometimes be regarded as Product, but Money as such has no value on its own but only as an instrument assigning value to Product.

I know people who would be puzzled by my claim that Money is not a Product and is without value on its own but only a multilateral medium for the transfer of products between different individuals or organizations. Yet if you try to understand the essence of Money, you will find that it is simply a tool to give value to product, a tool for accumulating wealth, a tool for moving products from one entity to another, or allocating its usage from present to future. Money is never a good or service that can be consumed, and so for practical purposes Money has no value by itself. Of course, for some people money as an object may be a source of pleasure. Some people immensely enjoy the sensation of holding banknotes, counting them over and over again, even spitting on their palms as they count. They enjoy the touch of money much as others enjoy holding a cup of tea in their hands on a cold wintry day and feeling the warmth permeate their frozen fingers. I shall not go into this phenomenon, though for this way of using Money is not the subject of my book.

Many economists like to claim that economics is a science and respectable as physics. I would call that a very pretentious attitude, but some of the models of physics can be used as good metaphors for a better understanding of economics. Here I shall take the liberty of using a basic physical distinction between two states of energy as a way of explaining how money works. Physicists speak of energy as always existing in one of two possible states: kinetic or potential. In my view money too is either in a kinetic state as what I call "money in circulation", or in a state of potential as **"money ready for circulation"**.

So how does all this work? A bachelor is about to play a game of billiards in a club, while on the other side of town a frustrated husband is walking into a shopping mall. Just at the moment the husband enters the mall, the balls are all neatly arranged on the billiard table waiting for the bachelor to start his game… As the bachelor's hand grasps the cue, ready for action, in the mall the husband's eye is caught by a beautiful golden necklace that has no real value for anybody, except for the husband, who has had a fight with his wife this morning and wants to make peace with her. The bachelor slides the cue through his fingers, imparting an external energy to the white ball, which in turn hits the group of colored balls; the balls are set rolling and hit each other until the energy wasted in the friction between the balls and the billiard table produces heat and stops the balls moving any further. At exactly that moment, the husband slides his credit card through the machine to pay 1000 dollars for the necklace, and almost immediately the Money reaches the jeweler's bank account. In his lunch-break the jeweler pops into the nearest shoe store and buys a pair of shoes for 500 dollars, and then with the remaining 500 dollars he repays the loan he originally took out with the bank to purchase the gold necklace from the artist who made it. In his turn the shoe-shop owner pays 250 dollars to his bank to cover the loan he took out to purchase the shoes from the shoemaker, and with the remaining 250 dollars he purchases a new suit for his own wedding, knowing nothing about the frustrated husband who started the chain reaction of Money and Product circulation.

The husband's irresponsible act in getting into a fight with his wife has set off a whole chain reaction of movement of products from the shops into the possession of new owners. In parallel the money has changed its potential, i.e. ready for circulation in the husband's wallet, to kinetic, when it left his wallet and was transferred to the jeweler, who transferred it to the shoe-shop owner and to the bank accounts and so on and so on.

Luckily, unlike in an atomic explosion, the chain reaction dies out naturally: not all the 1000 dollars that were put into circulation continue to circulate, but only 500 of them. The remaining 500 of the money in our story covers loans taken from a bank, and when these loans are repaid this money will be deposited in the bank vaults and so will revert from a kinetic to a potential state. Just the same would happen if the jeweler purchased the necklace for 500 dollars cash and after selling it for 1000 dollars used the extra 500 dollars to purchase a new necklace, and put the remaining 500 dollars in his pocket. The deposition of the money in the bank vault or in the jeweler's pocket has the same effect on the volume of money in circulation as the friction of the billiard balls on the billiard table has on their movement.

Of course, the jeweler might be an incorrigible optimist who believes he will be able to sell another new necklace for 1000 dollars the very next day, and then another and another on every subsequent day. After all, there is no lack of frustrated husbands who might walk through his shop door. So what if instead of paying back the loan of 500 US$ to the bank the jeweler had purchased two more new necklaces from the artist for 1000 dollars, and this had not been the end of the story because the shoe-shop owner was an optimistic type too, and so on and so on?

Could such optimism in shop owners cause a monetary blow-up? Well, the fact is that just as the chain reaction needed in an atomic bomb cannot happen out of the blue in nature (it needs a trigger in form of an exploding neutrons out of every cracked uranium atom, which if it occurred naturally would blow up the world), so an exponential increase in the volume of money in circulation cannot occur spontaneously. There are too many obstacles to an uncontrolled chain reaction of this kind. If you ask me what these obstacles are, my answer is that they arise from the tendency of Money to remain partly in the bank vault and only partly to continue to circulate.

The basic aim of this book is to explain two dimensions of

economics. The first concerns the separate worlds of Money and Product, and the way they circulate continuously in opposite circles with continual changes in the velocity of this circulation and in the volume of the money and the products circulating. The second concerns the ways limited resources are allocated by governments and financial institutions, or as in the metaphor I used at the beginning of this book, how to use a short blanket to try to keep both your feet and your shoulders warm.

As I hope you have understood, Product means everything you can buy for Money. This means merchandise or services, tangible and intangible assets, movable or immovable assets, real estate and dwellings. Perhaps surprisingly, financial assets like insurance, investments in investment funds and pension funds can also be products. Even certain forms of savings in the bank vaults can be considered products. This is because in these forms they are services supplying a feeling of security of future income that can itself be purchased for money.

The differences between financial investments in form of Money or other form of investment are not matters of distinction between Product and Money, but of differences in the degree of liquidity they have as Product, i.e. how fast and at what discount they can be converted from Product into Money ready for circulation.

To explain the phenomenon of the different levels of liquidity of different products, let's assume we have 10,000 dollars and we can choose between four different kinds of investment; The first is a five-year deposit of 10,000 dollars bringing annually 3%, subject to the condition that if the money is withdrawn during the five-year period, a 5 % penalty plus loss of all the interest accumulated on the deposit will be imposed. The second product is a new car, the third is a small apartment and the last is a highly specialized telescope. All these products can be purchased for 10,000 dollars. We also know that within a year we may suddenly have an urgent need for the 10,000 dollars, and the only way to get it will be by selling whichever of these products we finally decide to purchase. The question is what the best investment will be, taking into account the utility generated during this one year from the different investments.

The deposit seems the safest, because if we break it we will still get at least the 9500 dollars back, but the deposit does not give us any utility. The new car on the other hand will definitely lose much of its original price, but during the one year it will definitely supply a lot of enjoyment (utility). The telescope will not lose so much from its original purchase price while in our possession, but it may take quite some time to find the right buyer, who has an interest in astrology. And what about the apartment? Its liquidity will probably be the most complicated to predict. Generally the price of dwellings is more influenced by location than by physical state or appearance. The value of the "location" depends on many subjective parameters, which change over time in line with social trends. The apartment price may increase or decrease during the year.

From the financial point of view, all four products can be exchanged for Money ready for circulation; the only difference between them is how quickly this can be done and what "penalty" will be imposed on the Product at the moment of sale.

Money, if kept in the current accounts of commercial banks, can have different levels of liquidity. Some of these deposits are in the form of cash ready for immediate use, and others are fixed in short-term bank deposits. Yet there is a certain definite line between short-term deposits and long-term financial investments which makes the former Money and the latter Product and so forms a clear-cut division between Money and Product. And again, as I said earlier, Money itself is subdivided into kinetic money in circulation and potential money in the sense of money ready for circulation.

Now, to get a better understanding of the difference between Money in state of circulation compared to money in state of Product, let us try to imagine money as water in a canal flowing out of a huge reservoir containing many times more water than all the water in the canal.

This is a perfectly familiar image. But the oddity starts when we realize that this canal system has not only a sluice gate to control the volume of water flowing into the canal from the reservoir, but also a slope regulator that can slow down or speed up the velocity of the water-flow in the canal. The government is both the gatekeeper and the slope manipulator. It is obvious that the gate and the slope regulators influence the volume of the water flowing in the canal. If we substitute money for the water and the interest rate for the gate and slope regulator, with the gate representing long-term interest and the slope regulator representing short-term interest, we have a complete **Monetary System**.

The gate of the reservoir is the divider between *money out of circulation* (in the form of Product) and *money in circulation*. Another interesting physical property of shallow water is that it does not flow uniformly as one mass but its upper layer flows faster than its deeper layer. It is similar with Money. Only part of it is in a kinetic state while part of it is in its potential state, yet all of it is in circulation.

In a nutshell, Product is everything that Money can buy, while Money is the instrument that represents the value of Product without having any value by itself.

By definition, the *volume of product value in circulation* is always equal to the *volume of money in circulation*. This is because there is no product without a value in the form of a price expressed in units of money. Another way of putting this is that the *value of "the volume of product in circulation"* is always expressed as exactly the same *volume of money.*

Remember that a flower purchased in a flower shop is Product, while the same flower when you picked it in the meadow to give to your other half is not Product.

I feel that this beautiful painting of Franc Mark nicely expresses the circulation of Money and Product and their mutual friction and influence.

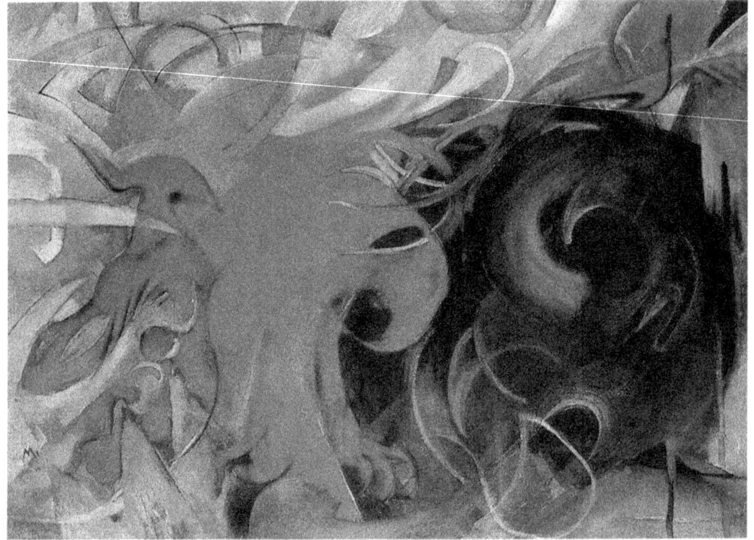

When is Product and Money in its potential state or out of circulation?

Money is usually deposited in saving accounts in commercial banks, while Product in its potential form is usually in storage, on the shop shelf, or in the process of production.

So when exactly are Money and Product in their kinetic state? At the moment when they are exchanged between buyer and seller. Don't be surprised that the kinetic state of Money and Product lasts at most for a few minutes. After all, it is very similar to what happens to energy. Energy builds up through long processes, like snow in the mountains that accumulates in the form of slabs of ice over a whole winter season or several seasons, or oil, accumulated during geological processes taking millions of years. When converted into kinetic energy this potential energy can disappear within a relatively short time compared to the time it took to accumulate.

Money as it changes its state from the potential to the Kinetic is the ultimate trigger and catalyst for the movement of Product from its potential to its kinetic state. In contrast to Money, Product is everything that has a quantitative and qualitative value definable in terms of Money, and which by its exchange for Money gives the purchaser its exact value relative to other products, also measured by Money. If a liter of milk costs a half-dollar and a liter of fuel costs a dollar, this represents the exact relative value of those two products. To repeat, Product as defined in this book is anything that can be purchased for money. That is why investments, whether monetary or non-monetary, such as company shares, real estate, or for some people even art, are also Product. On the other hand, money in circulation, whether in a potential or kinetic state, cannot be exchanged for money. You may object that money in one currency can be exchanged for money in another, and that large denomination notes can be exchanged for small change. But this is not something I define in this book as an act of purchase/sale, but simply as a tautological operation or redefinition of the same thing and same value in itself. (The commission taken by the broker for the "redefinition" is a payment for a service, or in our terms a Product.)

To use the metaphor from physics again, money like energy accumulates in its potential state for years, until finally in one moment it takes kinetic form, causing a parallel circulation of the product before it disappears from your account. It is not that it ceases to exist, any more than energy disappears when you burn it in your car or use it as electricity produced from a hydroelectric plant; it merely changes its state. Money changes its state from money in your savings account to money in the suppliers' savings account, or any other form of usage or deposit the supplier chooses. What about energy? The physicists have some brilliant answers to this, so go and ask them.

Having explained the two different states of Money and the metamorphosis it undergoes from its potential to its kinetic state, and how Money and Product mutually interact while in circulation, we can rightly ask the following question, "Is it in our human power to manage the volume of money and product in circulation?" Before starting to answer this very good question, I have to warn you that most of this book is about how the volume of money and volume of product value in circulation changes continually in the economy, and how these two phenomena are in a perpetual process of mutual synchronization. If you have not understood these connections fully yet, please be patient and I promise you it will be much clearer by the end of the book.

Money! Was it always as important as it is nowadays? Probably not. Before commerce was introduced into human life, homo sapiens could do very well without it. Commerce was probably the initial reason why humanity invented money, but even when money was already developing, while most people lived in villages they could still supply most of their needs for themselves. A peasant living in a village would not think of buying a frozen chicken in the village store. There were chickens in his yard and when he was sick his wife would slaughter one and make it into chicken soup. The only reason he needed money was to buy salt and other seasonings he could not produce. (Maybe this is the reason why in many ancient cultures salt was used as money). All the rest he could get by himself, or by bartering products with the local blacksmith and carpenter.

Urbanization was the second important step in the rise of money. It brought changes even to the peasant's life for he no longer needed to supply all his needs himself. He could buy the products he needed with money instead.

The third step in the development of Money came when it ceased to be physical. For a long period in history Money was made of gold, silver, or copper; later it became paper referring to the gold standard, meaning actual gold held somewhere; eventually it became just paper money deposited in commercial banks, and what changed hands between purchasers and sellers (despite the survival of coin for convenience) were different forms of paper, including banknotes or checks signed by the payer and given to the payee.

The fourth and most recent step in the form of money started with the computerization of Money. Payment these days is conducted either by credit card, direct internet transfer, or recently many other media, such as mobile phones, electronic vouchers etc.

All these progressive changes have not been mere technical changes, but have actually influenced the volume of money in circulation, as will be explained in the following chapters.

When Money changes its state, adding to or reducing the volume of money in circulation, it activates parallel processes of change in the volume of product value in circulation. As a private person, you can put your money into circulation when you have it somewhere in its potential state, but when you need money to purchase a product but don't have it in its potential state in a bank deposit or in your wallet, then the only way to get over the problem is to borrow money from someone else somewhere. And here we find another way of changing the state of money from potential to kinetic: it is called Credit. If not for credit, economic life would be very simple. Obsessive questions like "How am I going to cover my next mortgage payment?", "Why the hell did I use my credit card again?", or "I can't sleep since I borrowed that thousand dollars from Jimmy", would not exist. In fact this tool and curse called Credit was introduced very early in human history, when Money still took the form of words chiseled in stone tablets like this one more than 5000 years ago;

A Babylonian tablet (3100 BCE). It is part of a series of tablets that account for an order of 134,813 liters of barley to be delivered to the brewery at the temple of Inanna in Uruk over the course of 37 months

----

To talk about Money, we have to speak about governments, since down the ages it has been governments that have monopolized the right to be the sole creator of money and the defender of its value. Every government sees the creation of money as its prerogative but also its responsibility. Luckily, some European governments, either out of momentary inattention to their egotistic political interests or out of despair at the disastrous course of their predecessors' actions, decided voluntarily to cease to be governments as such when they agreed to create a united currency, the Euro. In the modern economy, the major contributor to changes in the *volume of money in circulation* is the government and its servant, the **Central Bank**. One of the best ways for a government to increase the *volume of money in circulation* is by creating a deficit. All a government has to do to create a deficit is to spend above its income. When a government does not possess enough money to cover its expenditure, it turns to the Central Bank, which prints new banknotes to cover the government deficit.

Yet even with the help of the Central Bank, if a government causes too serious a deficit and the *volume of money in circulation* rises substantially above the production capacity of the product producers and suppliers, the consequences for the economy can be grave. Remember that the *volume of money in circulation* has somehow to be equalized with the *volume of product value in circulation*, and so if the *volume of production* cannot be increased to cope with the *volume of money in circulation*, then this equalization can only come about by an increase in the price of the products. So sometimes, even the government cannot spend more than its income if it wants to avoid the kind of troubles you would have, if your expenses were higher than your income.

The government's budget, or in other words its annual plan for expenditure and tax income, is drawn up by government officials and submitted to the legislators for approval. Government expenses are comparable to your own personal expenses, which include payments for rent, food, electricity bills, interest on credit cards, your weekly drink with friends, etc. Taxes represent government income, and they are comparable to your monthly net income from wages, rents, interest on bank deposits dividends for your shares, or if you are lucky enough your profit from selling shares, etc. The difference between government and you is that a government can have expenses greater than its income for a relatively very long time without getting into trouble, whereas if your income fails to cover your expenses you will be in big trouble very fast.

The level of government spending over and above its income from taxes is called the **Government Deficit**. Why can a government run a deficit for much longer than a private person? The reason is that the general public has much greater faith in the government than in any private entity, including me, you and almost anybody else. This faith is mysterious, especially taking into account the well observed fact that governments practically never pay back their debts in full. At least that is what economists have thought for around 250 years, since Adam Smith, the very first real economist in human history wrote drily,

"When national debts have once been accumulated to a certain degree,

there is scarce, I believe, a single instance of their having been fairly and completely paid.

Nothing has changed since Adam Smith, and governments continue to create deficits, which mean expenditure not covered by collected taxes.

If we ordinary mortals don't have the money and nobody is ready to lend us any, we just cancel our shopping plans. Not so the government. Up its sleeve it has the wizard known as the Central Bank, which if asked can print money to cover the government's needs. By doing this, the Central Bank obviously increases the potential volume of money in circulation.

The capacity of the government with its central bank to print money makes the two of them more than just a product (service) provider or consumer like anybody else. It makes them jointly (the government and its instrument, the central bank) the major coordinator and decision-maker in the economy. If you get the feeling that the economy is in bad shape, and you are not earning what you deserve because someone has let you down, then you can always righteously blame the government.

If we want to talk about how the economy works, we have to talk about government, its tasks, functions, and what economic and political systems it uses and tools it has at its disposal to coordinate and influence the economy.

When I said earlier that Money in the bank vault and Money in your pocket are exactly the same in their potential state, I was only telling you a half-truth. The whole truth is that the bank does not just put the money you deposited in your bank account in the vault, but lends part of it to someone else, and charges interest on it. After all, even if you use the deposited money to make payments, most will be made by bank transfers, private checks, credit card payment or internet banking, and only very few will be made by direct cash banknote transfer. Imagining all the bank vaults as just one big vault, we can see that ultimately only a very small proportion of the deposited money leaves the bank vault as cash. This means that theoretically the bank could create an almost infinite volume of credit out of even a small deposit.

But don't worry. Not all your deposit can be used as credit: only about 90%! Any commercial bank (in the USA) is restricted by legislation and rules set by the Federal Reserve Bank to lending only up to this percentage of the money you deposited in your account. To enforce this rule the Federal Reserve Bank demands that commercial banks deposit 10% of their reserves in its vaults overnight, every night. (I wouldn't dare to suggest that the Federal Reserve Bank distrusts commercial banks, but I would hint that the central bankers want to show everybody who is the boss in the city). This rule is also one of the reasons why the volume of money in circulation cannot grow infinitely, as we noted earlier.

If you are still worried about ever getting the money you deposited in the bank back, I can reassure you: in more than 99.9999% of cases you will have no problem getting your money back, since it is unlikely that all the depositors will turn up at the bank at the same moment demanding their cash. And even if they did, which can happen when wildfire rumors lead depositors to panic about problems in a certain bank, there is still the Central Bank, which is obliged to act as the lender of last resort, and so will lend the commercial banks enough money to cope with an unexpected flood of cash withdrawals.

To understand the banking system, let us assume you deposited 100 dollars in your bank account, and the bank lends 90% of it to someone else. This is not the end of the story, because that credit of 90 dollars will be deposited in another bank account, and then another 81 dollars of that will be lent and deposited, and so on and on.

If you are still puzzled, remember that the borrowed 90 dollars will be deposited in someone else's bank account, even if not necessarily at your bank. The next step will be payment of the 90 dollars to a product provider, most probably again carried out by transfer from the borrower's bank account to the product provider's bank account.

Luckily this theoretically infinite recycling as credit of your 100 dollars deposited in the bank vault does not create an infinite *volume of money in circulation*, but only up to 900 dollars of the *potential volume of money in circulation*. And this maximum can only be reached on the supposition that the credit given by the bank on your deposit is constantly re -deposited in the checking accounts of some bank somewhere, and is subject to the full exploitation of the 90% limit on lending repeated over and over again.

Why 900? Let's calculate it; 90% of 100 is 90, 90% of 90 is 81.....so; 90+81+73+66+59+53+48+43+39+35+31+28+25+23+21+19+17+15+14+12 +11+10+9+8+7+6+6+5+5+4+4+3+3+3+3+3+2+2+2+2+1+1+1+1+1+1+1+1.. .now you have to believe me that if I go on and on and fill some 300 pages with 1s and then fractions then at the end the sum total will be 900.

This phenomenon is called the Multiplier, and it shows why in macroeconomic terms the money deposited in the banking system is very different from money deposited under your mattress or in your pocket. This is the case even if from your personal point of view there is no big difference between money in your pocket and in your current account. The point is that depositing money in the bank vault initially changes its state from kinetic to potential but that surprisingly, once it is lent to a borrower it increases the cumulative potential or kinetic *volume of money in circulation*.

Money in circulation has usually come straight out of deposits in the current account, but most of the money belonging to households and entities is not held in the current account but in a range of different forms of savings. If the money in all these forms of savings is added up, it actually comes to several times as much as the potential money in circulation in the form of cash or cash deposits in current accounts. This will not surprise you if I mention that the huge amount of money deposited in pension funds is also part of these savings.

One persistent challenge confronting economic and monetary policy is how to prevent this ocean of accumulated money from flooding the potential volume of money in circulation, or tidally draining it away. The answer is the **Interest Rate**.

How can the interest rate (like the dike-plugging Dutch boy in the story who stopped a flood with just one finger), stop the mountain of money bursting through from savings into *money in circulation* (potential or kinetic)? Well, try to imagine, you had two options: to purchase a new car for 10,000 dollars now, or get 20,000 dollars by lending your 10,000 dollars and waiting one year? Would you wait a year for your car purchase? Very probably yes. Of course this would presuppose a huge annual interest rate of 100% and no one will pay you that, but many people will postpone their new car purchase whenever the interest rate rises above its previous level.

I shall be trying to explain how this works in the following chapters. All I want to say at this stage of the book is that loans given by commercial banks are the major tool for transforming Money in its potential state to Money in its kinetic state and vice versa. Now, as is well-known, banks charge interest on loans, and of course the rate of interest is a major factor in our decisions to take a loan or not. Therefore, because the interest rate is relatively easily manipulated by the commercial banks and the Central Bank, *the volume of money in circulation* can be relatively easily squeezed or expanded. This relative flexibility of the *volume of money in circulation* is a phenomenon that I like to call the Speediness of Money.

3. Which is the bigger menace, Inflation or Deflation? (Introduction to Product)

While Money reacts very promptly to any change in interest rate, the responsiveness of Product to such external changes is a very different matter. If government officials, or CEOs, the Treasury Secretary or the Governor of the Central Bank, want to change the *volume of product value in circulation*, their only tools for achieving this are very clumsy, mostly imposed administratively, doubtful in effect and very delayed in any impact they may have.

The slow and limited response in the *volume of product value in circulation* to a changed economic environment is the result of its dependence on product production capacity. Product production capacity is itself dependent on inputs of different kinds from different sources. Just to mention some: human entrepreneurship, labor force, raw materials, energy, capital availability, technology, know-how in management, know-how in marketing, etc. All these resources tend to be either in over-supply and easily available, or else depleted and liable to scarcity in unpredictable ways. One day there is an abundance of them and nobody wants them, and the next day they are unobtainable at any price. To make matters even worse, if just one of the inputs needed to produce a product is in limited supply, this will be enough to cause an immediate scarcity of the finished products on the markets. You can produce millions of cars up to last detail without tires, but they will be useless if you have no rubber to make the tires.

This unreliability in the availability of the product or the components needed to produce it (which are also products) means that a product can suddenly appear in abundance and suddenly disappear in the same mysterious way. During the process of disappearance and reappearance the price of the product changes, sometimes gradually but often dramatically.

Dramatic change in product price occurs because the price is always determined by the most recent supplier-purchaser deal involving the product and not, as might be imagined, by the average price of the product in supplier-purchaser deals. To understand why, you have to bear in mind that in the free market there are many producers of the same product. Each of these producers has different production costs even if producing exactly the same product and each of the purchasers has different preferences for different products. Despite this, however, when selling the product on the market, every producer-supplier will sell his product for the maximum achievable price regardless of the production costs (assuming the producers-suppliers are all supplying the same product at the same quality.)

There is only one relevant price that the purchaser has to consider when deciding whether or not to buy the product, and this is the price at which a supplier sold that product to a purchaser in the most recent deal. This is also the only relevant product price considered by the supplier when deciding, on the basis of whether or not this price covers his production costs, whether or not to supply the product. (Do not forget, services also count as Product).

Depending on the price he can get for the product, every producer will decide whether or not to bother to produce it. If the price more than covers his production costs he will produce it, but if it is below production costs he will stop. If the product's market-price drops, many producers will find that their production costs are higher than the selling price and will immediately discontinue production. But then the product will naturally become scarcer on the market and its price will increase again, and with it production quotas. The opposite happens with demand: as the product's price increases, some of the potential buyers will decide not to purchase it. Then the product will become abundant on the market again and its price will decrease, and more buyers will become interested in buying it.

This is why the price of the product determines how many producers will produce how many products of the same kind. If the volume of a certain product is satisfactory for all the potential consumers at a particular price, then the demand and the supply may be said to have reached the **equilibrium-point price.** This is the price at which the volume of the product in circulation is just at the right level to fulfill the needs of the most recent consumer to purchase the product. This last product price agreed between the last purchaser and the last supplier will be applied to all further purchase-sale deals in the product until something changes the realities on the market.

To explain this perhaps counter-intuitive phenomenon of the establishment of the price by the last supplier-purchaser deal, I shall tell you the story of an island where there are 100 plumbers and 100 people who want to use 100 plumbers. This happy situation means that supply and demand are in absolute equilibrium, the price of plumbing is steady and everybody is perfectly satisfied. But suddenly a new customer appears: his name happens to be Mr.Hundred&One and he is what is known as the marginal customer for plumbing. Poor Mr.Hundred&One's toilet is broken and his house is in a big mess, and so he is willing to pay almost any price to get one of the 100 existing plumbers to come and repair it. The trouble is that right now the other existing islanders are in the same situation and are employing the existing hundred plumbers, one of which Mr. Hundred&One needs urgently. So they start to compete for the non-existent plumber 101 and this competition between customers necessarily causes an increase in the plumbers' prices.

After Mr.Hundred&One out of desperation has called all the plumbers in the island, every plumber in the island will get a feeling of increased self-importance, believe that he is the non-existent plumber 101 and so increase the price of plumbing to the skies. And so long as there continue to be more broken toilets on the island than plumbers, the broken toilet owners will compete between themselves for the service of the non-existent plumber 101. The indicative price, for which all the plumbers of the island will provide their service, will be the price of this deal between the customer named Mr.Hundred&One and the anonymous plumber out of the existing hundred plumbers.

When your toilet is broken there is no alternative to hiring a plumber (unless an unemployed economist changes his profession and retrains as a plumber at lightning speed), and so this situation will continue until a new plumber apprentice called Hundred&One Plumber is trained, which can take a long time. In the meantime, out of necessity, until a young plumbing apprentice acquires the skills to become the real Hundred&One Plumber, the broken toilet owners must either live with a stinking bathroom or find a non-existent Hundred&One Plumber among the existing hundred plumbers.

Why is it so? Because there is no real plumber called Hundred&One Plumber, but if there is a need for the non-existing Hundred&One Plumber all the plumbers will have the feeling that they are Hundred&One.

By the way, if the situation were the opposite, and there were only 99 owners of broken toilets seeking the services of the 100 plumbers, then one plumber, who happens to be called Hundred Plumber and needs the job or he will have no money to fill the fridge and his family will be hungry and angry with him, will reduce the price of his services below yesterday's price and again the price of this deal between the customer and Hundred plumber will become the indicative price for the services of all the plumbers on the island.

The conclusion is clear. The volume of product production cannot be changed by the magic wand of the government or a banker, even a central banker. Such a change has to be a synchronized change of many variables, such as the availability of an unemployed producer- supplier ready to be trained as plumber, a plumbing teacher, classroom, etc. Otherwise the change in the volume of product, in this case plumbing services, will not happen. This attribute of the product is what I like to call the "Laziness of Product".

The laziness is caused by the fact that the products have to be created by the whole chain of suppliers of the products. Ideally the product would react with perfect timing and perfect production quotas to cope with the challenge of changing economic circumstances caused by sudden change in the volume of the money in circulation, change of consumers' taste preferences or change in producers-suppliers' production costs. In fact, its response will rarely be perfectly synchronized with the "real need" created by a sudden change of the above mentioned parameters.

The unhappy lag in reactivity between the volume of money and product value in circulation causes continuous deviation from the equilibrium point between them, and disruption in the economy whenever the economic environment changes.

This recurrent disharmony between the *volume of money* and the *volume of value of products in circulation* can be very acute, in which case it is called an "economic crisis". But remember that by definition these two volumes are inseparable. The only way the Product Value can be expressed is by its unit volume multiplied by its price when circulating, and this has to be exactly equal to the Volume of Money in Circulation. If there is tendency for the Product and Money value to pull in different directions or move at different speeds, this means that the economy has lost its equilibrium point, and has to find its balance again one way or another.

There are three different ways in which this balance can be achieved:

Change in the volume of the products, by increased or decreased production and supply of the products by the producers-suppliers.
Change in the *volume of money in circulation.*
Change in the value of the products, by increase or decrease in the prices of the products.

In an economy where increase in the *volume of money in circulation* comes prior to any increase of *volume of product value in circulation*, production has a tendency to expand its volume to catch up with the higher *volume of money in the circulation*. But production capacities to increase the volume of production are not always available. If this is the case, the only way to equalize the two rotating items, the Money and the Product, is by change the value relationship between them, or in other words change in the price of the products.

Since the total *volume of the value of products* and the total *volume of money* circulating in the economy have to be equal, there have to be equalizing processes that bring these two variables into perfect equality and resolve the tension between the Speediness of Money and the Laziness of Product. There are two equalizers with very frightening names. One is called **Inflation** and the other **Deflation**. To me, deflation sounds somehow more masculine than Inflation, but (believe me) both of them are very formidable warriors, and sometimes they even join forces in an alliance called "Stagflation".

The deflation process is activated when the total volume of the value of products in circulation has a tendency to be higher than the total volume of the money in circulation. You may say, "What's the big deal? Why do we need to fear deflation? Just reduce the product prices and everything will fall into place!" That is easy to say but hard to do, because the existing prices in the economy sustain a whole system of employers who pay wages to their employees, who produce products that are sold for profit to the shopkeepers, who sell them for profit to consumers.

This whole process of creating the final product that ultimately reaches the consumer, comprises a whole sequence of phases, with each production phase adding some additional value to the previous production phase. This is the case whether the product is a non-material service, or merchandise created out of raw material. To prevent any misunderstanding, I must emphasize again and again that production is not only material production in factories or workshops, but also supply of services, like those of shopkeepers, marketers, deliverers but also bankers, or any other entities directly or indirectly involved in getting a final product to the consumer and paid for their service.

This production process involves a whole chain of participants, with each of them generating a certain **Added Value,** (unless the producers of the product are losing money in the process). **This added value is created in each step of the production process, where it equals the price for which the product is sold to the next stage of the production process, minus the cumulative cost of all the components needed to create the product in the previous stages of the production chain.**

When eventually the product reaches its final state and is sold to the consumer, the product cost includes all the added value accumulated up to the final state of the product. In fact the added value of the product represents the total net income generated during the product production process by all the individuals or entities that participated in the production process. This net income includes all the wages and capital income in the form of profit and interest, right fees, publishing rights, royalties, rents, etc.

All these participants in the process of creation of the Product are used to getting a share of this added value or **Net Income,** and none of them wants to give up "their" accustomed share of the reward, even if storm clouds of Deflation are looming over them. This inflexibility, caused by the general propensity of people to act egoistically, means a tendency to stick to the level of income achieved in the past. As a socio-economic phenomenon it is the reason for many discrepancies in the economy.

I believe that the reason for this economic conservatism is competitiveness between the different participants in the production process. Everyone wants to increase his share on the added value created in the production process and nobody wants to reduce his share of it, or in other words nobody wants to be a loser in the process even if the economic realities demand it. This is the reason why workers strike for unrealistic wages, even though such rises would not leave enough added value to enable the employer, entrepreneurs, creditors, sub-suppliers and other elements in the production chain to sustain their business activity.

On the other hand, it is also the reason for unrealistic increases in the price of products at times when the volume of money in circulation is insufficient to finance the whole volume of value of products in circulation potentially available in the economy. This continuous competition between the segmented participants in the creation of added value (the producer and the merchant, the employer and employee, the capital owner and the worker) for bigger and bigger shares of the common cake seems to be an integral part of the economic system. In times of prosperity the participants in the creation of added value tend to compete to achieve as big a slice as possible of the additional added value generated, while in times of difficulty and economic depression they try to stick to what they have secured in the past.

This strategy of sticking to what was achieved in the past can work in normal times, but when real Deflation approaches it may have a devastating effect.

The first sign of real Deflation is when first the final products, then the products in the production process, and finally the raw materials, start to pile up on the production floor. The Production Manager starts to yell at the Marketing Manager to clear the finished products from the production floors so he can continue his production as planned. The Marketing Manager retorts that last month's product is still piled right up to the ceilings in the final product stores and from his point of view production should be halted altogether. The Production Manager loudly inquires what he should do with all the raw materials that the suppliers are continuously sending him, and even more, what he should do with all the workers in production. This goes on and on until finally the Financial Manager arrives and starts to yell at both of them that the **Cash Flow** is negative, that there is no finance for all this junk piling up everywhere, and that the banks are already threatening to cut off the credit line.

Nobody can be indifferent to this kind of argument, for everybody knows that these three words; "Negative Cash Flow", mean something very serious and dangerous; last time the Cash Flow was Negative, it meant that payments to some suppliers, employees and even the managers' salaries had to be halved, that prices had to be renegotiated with suppliers, and wages with employees, and the process was very tiresome and unpleasant.

So finally they all sit down in the General Manager's office and the Financial Manager explains to the Production and the Marketing Manager that if the Cash Flow continues to be negative, the credit line the bank agreed to give to the producer will dry up, and if there is no credit there will be no money either for raw materials or for wages. And so they decide to decrease the rate of production. First they stop buying raw materials. Later, when the Marketing Manager fails to bring in the new orders he promised to find at the last meeting with the General Manager, they send the workers on forced vacation for two weeks... And later, when the orders for new products still don't arrive, they may have to lay off some of the workers.

If you thought that getting rid of existing production capacity was no more problematic than throwing inedible out-of-date food from the fridge, the description above should give you a slightly more realistic understanding of what happens when a reduction in the volume of production is required in a relatively short time frame.

Inflation, on the other hand, arises when the volume of value of product in circulation is lower than the *volume of money in circulation*. In the modern economy Inflation is constant and continuous because all governments are afraid of Deflation (angry unemployed voters!) and to be on the safe side they prefer to increase the *volume of money in circulation* (relatively easily done as we have said before), and accept the increase in price levels as a lesser evil. In any case, an increase in the *volume of money in circulation* does not necessarily cause inflation. If there are enough potential production resources, it can create economic growth.

Economic Growth is increase in the volume of product in its kinetic and potential state, or in other words either in circulation or ready for circulation. The result of economic growth is increased wealth, in the form of more accumulated products in their potential or kinetic state.

According to the definitions in this book, Wealth is Product and/or Money accumulated in its potential state. It can be in the form of assets, tangible or intangible. Or in other words wealth is accumulated cash money, savings deposits or current account deposits in a state of potential circulation, and/or everything we define in this book as product potentially ready for circulation.

To explain this difficult definition I would like to ask you a riddle;

Johnny and Bobby both have 20,000 dollars in their wallets. Bobby decides to purchase a new car, while Johnny keeps hold of his 20,000 dollars. After a month they meet in the pub and after couple of beers they start to argue about which of them is wealthier, Bobby with his brand new shiny car or Johnny with his 20,000 dollars still tucked in his wallet?

If you were around and they asked you, probably you would say they were equally wealthy since Johnny could always go out and buy the same new car the next day. But if I were sitting next to them, and still sober, I would say Johnny is the wealthier. The next day he could buy the same new car as Bobby, or keep his 20,000 dollars. On the other hand, as I am sure you should know, second-hand cars sell for much lower prices than brand new ones, so if Bobby sold his car the next day he would get less for it than he originally paid for it.

You ought now to agree with me that whatever form wealth takes it is always a potential value, while once it is consumed stops being wealth.

Another way to define wealth: All the Money in a kinetic state in circulation or ready for circulation plus the Money in a potential state accumulated in the "Financial Reservoir". In an ideal economy this "Financial Reservoir" should be backed by the accumulated "Product creation capacity". (I intentionally don't use the world production capacity but creation capacity, to differentiate between them.)

For accumulated Money or Product to change its state from potential to kinetic, the owner of the wealth must decide to transform it from product or money ready for circulation to Money and Product in circulation. How does this happen? Easy: if for example, you decide to spend the pension fund you saved for your whole life on enjoying your life before you get old, you will change the money from its state as product to its potential state and then to its kinetic state. The same will happen when you sell the house you inherited from your grand - grandfather and use the money for a pleasure trip to Las Vegas.

To return to Inflation or price increase, economists have developed several tools to measure increase in prices, and these tools are known as **Price Indexes**. They can measure price change over the whole economy, but also just specific product prices, like housing prices for example. One of the most useful Price Indexes is the Consumer Price Index, which measures change in the cost of an average person's basket of expenses.

Have you ever asked yourself why the index of prices only ever rises? Did you realize that the Consumer Price Index had doubled in the last 25 years? If you don't believe me, try to recall how much you paid 25 years ago for a soda. If you are too young to remember, forget it.

Like deflation, inflation has its very dark side. It brings uncertainty into the economy: the holder of money in bank deposits or in other forms of savings cannot be sure of the future value of his deposit. This insecurity in regard to the future value of the savings reduces his propensity to save and automatically increases his spending right now. This decline of saving during inflation adds to the volume of money in circulation and so exacerbates the inflationary trend.

The change in people's propensity to save, and with it their spending behavior, tends to undermine their optimal utilization of personal resources. Decreasing saving habits among the people can also be expressed as the switching of resources from future use to use today, from investment to consumption, and inevitably has a negative impact on real economic development in the future.

As I said at the beginning of the book, the economic game is all about correct allocation of resources (remember the short blanket?). Inflation interferes with this resource allocation and seriously distorts it. The activities of entrepreneurs become more and more focused on manipulating Money and less and less on creating Product.

If you have ever lived in a country with a real Inflation – and I mean dramatic inflation, as in South America - then you probably know that a period of steep Inflation is the best time for financial experts and speculators to make money out of money. These are times when financial managers get higher wages in the production company than production managers, and this means you have more and more volume of money, and against it less and less volume of product value in circulation.

At times of Inflation economists have their hands full creating two price index systems to monitor economic processes and data, i.e. the real price system and the nominal price system. Nominal prices are the prices for which the shops sell their Products, whereas real -term prices are prices recalculated according to some anchor, which is either a foreign currency or some historical price level. The economist needs the real term prices to try to figure out what is really going on in the economy, and the merchants and producers need them to calculate prices relative to other prices.

The process of Inflation usually starts with a general increase in prices, which after a while prompts the unions to complain that wages are ceasing to cover the daily expenses of employees. Then pensioners and the other sectors of society that live on social security payments start to protest. Last but not least the banks react, by increasing interest rates to keep them above the level of the price increase level.

Have you ever asked yourself why at times of increased rate of inflation the interest rate rises too? What would happen if the interest rate were below the rate of inflation? When inflation prevails in the economy and the interest paid on savings is below the level of the price increase, financial assets lose a proportion of their real value. To take an example:, suppose that a year ago you had 1000 dollars and wanted to buy a new home cinema system costing exactly 1050 dollars. Not wanting to take out a loan, you had deposited 1000 dollars in the bank for 5% interest with the intention of waiting patiently until the end of the year when you would be able to purchase the home cinema system. But over the year the inflation rate has been 10%. At the end of the year you find that the home cinema price has increased exactly in line with the general price index, so its value is now 10% more and it costs 1155 dollars. So if at the beginning of the year you needed an extra 50 dollars to purchase the set, now, since you have only 1050 dollars, you need an additional 105 dollars to buy it. On the other hand if at the beginning of the year you had treated yourself to the set immediately by borrowing 1050 dollars at 5% interest rate, at the end of the year the value of your set would have been 1155, and your debt to the bank would be 1102.50 dollars. So you would have made a profit of 52.5 dollars by taking the loan. The prospective profit to be made out of borrowing if the interest rate is below the price increase rate would create an increased demand for bank credit, while on the other hand depositors would be motivated to withdraw their deposits from the bank vaults. To avoid being overwhelmed by borrowers asking for credit and depositors asking to withdraw their deposits, the banks must keep the interest rate above the inflation rate.

Then, as production costs rise, the exporters complain that their competitiveness against other producers from other countries has been damaged and they will have to lay off some of the workforce unless a compensatory adjustment is made. It is also common knowledge that without exports no foreign currency will be available to purchase the import commodities necessary for the economy. So the currency is devalued. But then all the imported goods that have to be bought for foreign currency become more expensive and the round of price increases starts all over again.

Because the different segments of the production chain have lost confidence in the stability of the price system, the new round of price increase will necessarily be higher than the previous one. As expectations of further price increase among the people mount, everybody wants to be compensated not only for the last price increase, but also for the expected next price increase, which they believe will be higher than the last one. To secure their position, all the participants in the society ask for exaggerated price and wage increases. By this stage the price increase is gathering extra momentum and is driven by expectations rather than by realities. And the expectations tend to be self-fulfilling.

And so as the spiral winds ever upwards, first the employers and the employees and last the institutions of social benefits like social security, pension funds etc., create a system of indexation based on an agreed anchor for prices, wages, tariffs, fees, charges, expenses, fares, premiums, rates, tolls, whatever...

At first the indexed raises occur every quarter, but then they happen every month and at the end every week. Theoretically everybody - the employees, the pensioners, the exporters and even the producers - should get proportionately the same progressive increases in income, but that does not happen in practice because it is impossible for people to keep their bearings in the avalanche of numbers. Those with a strong negotiating position get more and the others get less. Some economic entities even cease to exist, either because they lack the means to cope with the frequent price increase, or because they just don't understand what is going on around them.

At a certain stage the prices start to rocket exponentially, and this stage is called Hyperinflation. In Hyperinflation the prices change daily until nobody has any remaining sense of the relative value of products, for **Money has lost its major function as the supreme measurer of the value of Product price.** During hyperinflation if you ask someone how much a loaf of bread costs he will probably just shrug, or if he is more polite he will tell you the price in a foreign currency. This is the stage at which the market starts looking for an anchor for measuring prices other than the local currency. Usually the anchor is a stable foreign currency, for example the dollar, or some other form of indexation.

This image of a spiral is not an exact representation of the inflation spiral, but it is beautiful and so I shall use it anyway.

I once knew a very nice old man whose name was Salman. He inherited a petrol station from his grandfather and when Britain was still a great empire he used to supply fuel for trucks of the British colonial army. Then the British Empire collapsed and the British went away, but he continued

to supply fuel to big trucks on the same terms as under the British —
offering three months of interest-free credit. This worked wonderfully for
quite a long time, but as he became older and less adaptable, and a
spiral-like dance of inflation started in the new country that had emerged
from the wreck of the British Empire, Salman failed to see what was
happening. He did not realize anything was wrong, especially when he
started to sell more fuel than ever before, and even after midnight the
trucks were still queuing up in front of his pump.

Blindly attached to the old principle he had once heard from his
grandfather, "never let a customer down", he continued to sell more and
more fuel, always with three months of interest-free credit. Then one day
he found he didn't have enough money left to fill the fuel station
underground tanks. That was the end of his story but not the end of the
Inflation, which has a tendency to run out of control.

To summarize, the defaults caused by hyper-inflation leads to
deformation of the business climate. The most striking and unmistakable
sign of this deformation is disproportionate expansion of the financial
sector, whose services are in increasing demand from individuals and
entities trying to avoid the costs of Inflation. Inflation leads to
inconsistencies in the relative prices of different products and uncertainty
about future price levels. It complicates the business environment and
makes the decision-making process hard, thereby decreasing economic
efficiency. It causes unintentional redistributions of wealth by penalizing
the owners of assets and income with a value not indexed to the price
rise, and rewarding those whose possessions and income are indexed. It
distorts the tax system by disrupting the accounting system, and finally,
people like Salman tend to fall into the trap of misunderstanding the
financial processes and the difference between the nominal and real
value of product prices.

This instability in the distribution of the wealth among the population
causes a great deal of trauma. You have to remember that it is much less
traumatic to stay poor than to become poor when you used to be rich.

(This is why when the Wall Street Crash happened in 1929, many brokers jumped from high windows, but no beggar thought about committing suicide because of lack of money.)

So now we are back at our first question: Which comes first, the Money or the Product? And in the modern economy it is Money with its speediness that tends to come first. But it was not always like this. In the past when Money was minted out of precious metal, if the metal was plentiful because of the discovery of new golden or silver mines then Inflation reared its head, but if the mines become depleted the opposite process of Deflation set in.

As I explained above, the *volume of money in circulation* at its optimal equilibrium point is equal to the *volume of product value in circulation*. It is very unlikely that the volume of value of precious metals available for minting money could ever be exactly the right volume of money in circulation needed to secure the *volume of product value in circulation* at full employment. Only at the end of nineteenth century did economists start to realize that money should represent the *volume of product value in circulation* rather than the volume of value of some precious metal, and it still took them almost a century longer to uncouple Money from the volume of gold deposited in the Central Bank vault.

The best example of total misunderstanding of the problem expressed in our question; "Which comes first, Money or Product?" with disastrous historical consequences, is 16th -century Spain. The gold and silver mines of the new Spanish colonies in South America gave Spain what seemed to all an enormous economic advantage - unending treasure to fund the Spanish dream of hegemony over Europe and the imposition of strict Catholicism on the English, Dutch, and French.

Like most of the world, since Roman times and even earlier Europe had used money made of precious metals, mainly gold and silver, which being scarce meant it was relatively easy to enforce a monopoly on their mining. The kings strictly guarded their right to mint coins out of it (the government monopoly on money creation). Whenever over-production of coins caused Inflation, leading to resentment among the peasants and the general public, and even worse, anger among the soldiers who fought their holy and unholy wars, the kings used to chop off the hands of the coinage minters, blaming them for cheating and adding too much cheap tin to the "golden" coins.

By coincidence, in the last decade of the 15th century, just at the point when the depletion of golden and silver mines in Europe reached its peak, and the deficit of volume of money in circulation as compared to Product volume created reality that in this book we call "Product coming first", the Spanish kicked the last Muslims out of Granada (and then out of inertia the Jews too). Released from the now completed task of "Reconquering" Spain, the Spanish queen now found time to look enviously at her neighbors across the border in Portugal, which had a fleet of ships already crisscrossing the Atlantic Ocean and bringing riches to the country and its king. So she sent out her own ships with Christopher Columbus (some say Columbus was one of the Jews who had fled Spain a few years earlier for Italy, after he was forced to convert to Christianity).

The discovery of America brought a huge flow of gold and silver to Spain, and suddenly the Spanish economy was transformed from a scarce-money economy into a plenty-of-money economy. But then came Christopher Columbus's revenge, or as I like to call it, "lottery winner syndrome". In fact the money had an increasingly negative effect on Spanish production. The Spanish monarch concentrated mainly on importing gold and silver to be turned into coin to fund wars all over Europe. This huge increase in gold and silver coin caused inflation in Spain itself and made Spanish products too expensive. Meanwhile the products of the French, Dutch and English, whose economies were still suffering a squeeze on the volume of money in circulation and so a depressed domestic demand for their own products production capacity, remained relatively cheap, and so successfully penetrated onto the Spanish market. Yes these were the very French, Dutch and English that Spain tried unsuccessfully to subordinate and convert to strict Catholicism.

Eventually then, all the gold and silver imported from the Spanish colonies helped not Spain but its enemies, whose economies, under pressure of scarcity of money in circulation, continued to over-produce products that their own population could not consume for lack of cash, and exported them to Spain where the cash was available. Combined with the development of cheaply produced new goods like the trade in black slaves from Africa and profitable new services like piracy and robbery of Spanish ships, all this meant that the Spanish lost their position of influence in Europe together with their economic prosperity. It was a loss from which Spain was not to recover until modern times.

As for Christopher Columbus, like his contemporaries he probably had no idea of the importance of the question, "Which comes first, Money or Product?" Luckily for him, he didn't know the correct size of the globe either, since he never read Eratosthenes who had calculated it correctly more than 1000 years earlier. If he had, he would never have hoped to reach India by crossing the Atlantic, the Native Americans would never have been called Indians, and John Wayne might never have become a Hollywood star. On the other hand, Christopher Columbus did know something about eggs. When some Spanish courtiers belittled his achievement in finding America he took out an egg and asked them "Who can make this egg stand on its end?"

4. What a beautiful island we used to have

In the preceding chapter we used the example of an island with plumbers and plumbers' customers. Now let us imagine an economy on another island, which has some of the key elements we have described but not much else! It has no ports, no airports, and not even a government, but just a central banker, private bankers and economically active population, who are producing and trading products by exchanging them for money. This island state has no history, no myths, no national ethos, and no allies, whether boring and burdensome, supportive or demanding. Even the islanders' native language is used only inside their houses in total privacy; in public they communicate in Esperanto, which by common consent can never be used for poetry or prose but only for legal contracts, legislation and scientific publications, to prevent any irrational attachment to it. (I wonder what they would make of pseudo popular - science publications like this book, which offers facts that are not always precise, draws conclusions that are also not always correct, and spices its prose with stories that pretend to be funny).

Anyway, one day the people of the island boldly decided to build ports and airports, and eventually a bridge across the channel separating it from the Mainland. This will bring the island's history as a self-enclosed economy to an end, for it will now be connected to the mainland economy. Those islanders who wanted the bridge said it would allow them to send their products across the bridge and import different products or even the same products, (even though this may seem not to make much sense, it is what often actually happens). And not only would products be transferred across the bridge, but money too. Some islanders opposing the bridge predicted that transferring money and product across the bridge would eventually attract anti-globalization radicals, who would litter the island's streets with beer cans, damage walls and up-end dustbins on policemen's heads!

The merchants discovered very fast that across the bridge in the Mainland there was an economy with its own currency called the dollar rather than the pound sterling used in the island. They found that for one pound they could get two dollars, and that the fish from the other side of the bay, which was just as good as the fish on the Island coasts, cost one dollar each, while the island fishermen were selling it for a pound. What could be easier and more profitable than to exchange pounds for dollars and import fish from the mainland? That is exactly what the merchants started to do. Consequently the price of fish on the island went down and everybody was happy... except for the fisherman who suddenly couldn't sell their fish for the same price as before. The fisherman were particularly irritated about the merchants' new ad slogan for the imported fish: "Freshy, Cheapy, Mainlandy!". "Surely" grumbled the fishermen, "everyone knows that the island's fish are as good as the mainland's. And not even all that much more expensive – they only cost double".

Feeling neglected by their fellow-islanders, the fishermen held a meeting and decided to organize a demonstration on the Island Main Square and even invite some anti -globalization activists from the mainland, hoping for support in their rally against the opening up of the economy.

With their placards and slogans the island's fishermen reminded the islanders what a perfect life they used to have before the bridge and the ports were built. For all those years – the fishermen pointed out - they had faithfully supplied the islanders with fish, plenty of fish... so what if was for double the price of fish today? That was a mere detail! They shouted and chanted patriotic slogans, condemning the unpatriotic behavior of the other citizens of the island and above all those selfish merchants who were encouraging consumption of the cheaper mainland fish instead of the local fish. They lamented that they had been betrayed by their fellow citizens, and cruelly abandoned after so many years of devoted toil. Was not the Island Fish Corporation a precious asset belonging to the whole island and not just the fisherman? What was going to happen if the mainlanders decided one day to stop the supply of the fish to the islanders? Who if not the island's fishermen would be on hand to meet all the islanders' fish needs even at double the price?

Yet none of these arguments convinced the others. As it turned out the anti-globalization activists didn't make it to the meeting on the square. They were too busy demonstrating against the MMF and IMF and EZMF, whose joint super-conference in the mainland capital happily coincided with the annual beer festival when beer is served free in litter bins. So the fishermen, disappointed, started to look for a better solution to their troubles than protest meetings.

After a while they realized that the nets on the island cost half a pound sterling each because of a unique knotting technique used there, while on the mainland they cost only 2 dollars. The fishermen were also skilled at weaving fishing nets, so now they started to make nets instead of going to fish every night. And soon, once the dust in the island's square had settled, the islanders realized that while before the bridge was built they had needed one and a half pounds for one net and one fish, now they could purchase an islander net for a half pound and a mainlander fish for one dollar and together the products would cost just one pound.

Do you still support anti-globalizers? If so you are not alone. It could easily be 40 years before the fishermen stop speaking nostalgically of the wonderful moonlight at 3 o'clock at night, when they used to get up and jump into their boats, heading for the rippling waters of the bay. Just like this:

If you are still asking why we need any buying and selling across the bridge, the answer can be found once again in the laws of physics. Do you remember the experiment with communicating vessels in the physics lab? When a fluid is poured into a set of containers connected along their bases, it will eventually balance out at the same level in all of the containers regardless of their shapes and volumes. If additional liquid is added to one vessel, the liquid will again find a new equal level in all the connected vessels. Well, the ports and the bridge do exactly the same for connected economies as the tubes do for the connected lab vessels, just with the difference that in the laboratory it's the liquid that goes from one vessel to the others through the tube and reaches an even level in all of them, while in the countries linked by international commerce it's the price level that gets equalized. To stop it happening you have to prevent the building of bridges and ports, and so you end up with a standard of living like North Korea's. After this explanation you will not be surprised that a bottle of coke costs almost the same in New York as in Kuala Lumpur. Where the hell is Kuala Lumpur?

But what happens if it's not only the price of fish that is higher on the island than on the mainland, but also the price of nets and all the other products the islanders produce and consume? Now both the fisherman and fishnet weavers will have difficulty finding a job. Since more and more pounds get exchanged for dollars to purchase products from the mainland, the volume of money in circulation in the island drops. For a little while, the standard of living of the population rises as a result of the cheap imports, but the island's production capacity shrinks and eventually this causes unemployment. Soon the people of the island realize that even though the fish is now cheaper, they don't have the money to purchase it. As we know, Deflation is just around the corner.

You are probably already asking where the islanders are going to get the dollars to buy all these products from the mainland. You are right to ask. After all, the islanders have nothing to sell the mainlanders but still need dollars to buy the mainlanders' products. At first they can exchange their sterling for dollars, but very soon the mainlanders realize that they can't purchase anything with sterling – not fish, nor nets, nor anything else -- so who needs these pounds sterling anyway?

Before the opening of the bridge, only very few mainlanders needed sterling and even fewer islanders needed dollars. If any exchange of currency occurred at all it was an oddity and not an everyday experience. Most of the exchangers back then were banknote collectors not merchants. Way back in the past it had been decided, for some long forgotten reason, that one pound sterling could be exchanged for two dollars, and this was the exchange rate between the two currencies at the moment the island and the mainland were connected.

As the island opened up to the mainland, and more and more dollars were needed to purchase the mainland's fish, the dollar-bill collectors ceased to have interest in sterling bills. And so as more and more island merchants crossed the bridge loaded with sterling bills they found that soon no money dealer was ready to change two dollar bills for one sterling bill. They offered less and less for it. This process of value depreciation of the pound against the dollar continued until the price of the fish caught by the island fisherman equaled the price of fish caught by the mainland fishermen.

When the exchange rate was re-stabilized at one dollar to one pound sterling, the islanders announced that this act, called Currency Devaluation, was going to save the island's fishermen and bring prosperity to the island's net weavers as well. The island fish still cost one pound sterling but before the building of the bridge and port one pound had been convertible to two dollars, and now it was just one dollar to one pound sterling; this meant that each fish caught by the island fishermen cost the same one dollar or pound sterling as the fish caught by mainlanders. It must now be clear enough how devaluation of currency brings change in the product prices on the island relative to the product prices of the mainland, despite the fact that the local prices on the domestic market of the island and the mainland have not changed at all.

Another consequence of the devaluation is that while before devaluation the nets woven by the island weavers were equal in price to those of the mainland net weavers, the island nets will suddenly be much cheaper, and naturally the mainland fisherman will now buy their nets only from the islanders.

Of course, even though the island and mainland fish now cost the same, there will be islanders who prefer the special flavor of mainland fish, and some mainlanders who prefer the island fish (to the great annoyance of the mainlander fishermen!). So the island fish now start to be sold to the islanders again, as well as some mainlanders. The happy result is that the island fishermen can return with their boats to the bay at three o'clock in the morning, and no longer feel the need to demonstrate on the island square.

One day, the islander fishermen will get lucky and their fish will be introduced as a specialty item on the menu of a very expensive mainland restaurant. The restaurant owner will be loud in his praises of the island fish as much tastier than mainlanders' fish, and so eating island fish will become a fashion and hallmark of good taste and prestige among the mainlanders. One of the mainland celebrities will talk about his great adventure spending a whole night on an island fishing boat with an authentic islander fisherman, and in his cultural column in the Mainland Sunday News he will contrast the noble island fishermen with the commonplace mainland fishermen, who are always using bad language whenever their nets catch on rocks at the bottom of the bay. But how the islanders start to prosper when their fish acquire a name as being a better product than the mainlander's fish is a different story, and one I shall have to leave for a different book.

You may now be thinking that Devaluation has put everything right on the island and the mainland, but this is not quite so. The change in the currency exchange rate offers the potential for the island to export its products to the mainland, but has many side effects. The first is an increase in the price of fish on the island: with one pound sterling now equal to one dollar, the mainland fish, which before devaluation cost a half-pound-sterling, will cost one pound sterling.

On the other hand, if before the devaluation the mainlanders could buy an island -made net for one dollar, i.e. half a pound sterling for the islanders, now they can purchase it for only half a dollar. This angers the mainland net-weavers, whose products are now too expensive. As we can see, the devaluation solves the problem of the unbalanced relative prices of fish between the mainland and the island, but creates a problem with the net prices. The conclusion: after the building of a bridge for free movement of goods across the bay, the prices of the nets and the fish will equalize, either by devaluation of the island's sterling or by a de crease in the island production costs and profit expectations, but both these processes will create many angry people on the island and on the mainland as well.

The island citizens might not, of course, want to devalue their sterling against the dollar at all, whatever their reasons. Some may consider it a matter of patriotic pride and honor for one pound to be more valuable than one dollar (this would of course be counter to our assumption that the islanders are absolutely rational). The mainlanders might also not want to change the exchange rate of the dollar to the pound sterling, since the existing rate enables them to sell the islanders the fish surplus that they can't consume themselves and don't want to turn into pickled or smoked fish because that is so costly and unappealing. They therefore decide to help the islanders purchase their products by lending them dollars to finance the import of fish and nets from the mainland. In this case the island will have a trade deficit with the mainland, which means that the islanders will consume more than they produce, while the mainlanders will be in the exactly opposite situation. Economists call this difference between the island's production and consumption a **"trade deficit"** and the opposite phenomenon on the mainland a **"trade surplus"**.

The trade deficit may look like a good deal for the islanders; after all, if they can import the cheap mainland fish, and finance it with the mainlander's money, their own fishermen will have no need to get up early in the morning to do the hard work of fishing themselves. But there is no way the island can sustain a trade deficit for any length of time, unless the lender of the dollars that they need to purchase the mainland fish is willing to keep on lending. Countries with a continuous trade deficit are heavily indebted to other countries, but a trade deficit will usually be a short-term matter because nobody likes to give loans if the return on them is not secure. At the end of the day, when the mainlanders realize that the islanders' debts are too high ever to be paid back, they will stop financing the trade deficit, and then devaluation of the sterling against the dollar will be inevitable.

But once a trade deficit has arisen and the lender has dipped out, the economic problem will be much greater than at the time when the bridge had just been built and opened. Now the island fisherman and their net-weavers will have to produce enough fish and nets not only to cover the needs of the islanders but also to cover the repayment of the debt created by the trade deficit. So it will not be enough just to overcome the trade deficit, but a trade surplus will have to be generated as well. Unfortunately, the islanders discover to their consternation that during the period of the island's trade deficit policy, some island fisherman have lost most of their fishing skills while the net-weavers have forgotten how to weave nets. So now they can hardly cover the needs of the island itself for the products, still less create surpluses needed to pay back the loans they took from the mainland.

It might have been very different if the loans the island took from the mainland had been invested in the fish industry, creating fish ponds for breeding the freshwater fish demanded by the mainlanders rather than being spent on the consumption of fish imported from the mainland. But it's no use crying over spilt milk and in the coming years the islanders will just have to increase their fishing and the net-weaving production, eat less fish and supplement their diet with seaweed, which is very abundant on the open ocean side of the island. The fishermen will sell part of the fish catch on the mainland for a reduced price. Learning from the past, they will use the dollars received from the mainlanders to create fishponds to breed freshwater fish rather than to support their own eating habits. Let us hope they continue this policy until the fish ponds start to produce these delicious fish, which are mostly sold to the mainlanders. Then one day a new generation of islanders invent a new kind of cookies made from seaweed, which proves very successful on the mainland. Now the islanders are able not only to repay their debts but also to create a big surplus, and so the tables are turned and it is the mainland that is beginning to run up a trade deficit.

The lesson from this short economic history of the island's policy is that if the people of the island have a strong feeling of cohesion, and readiness to sacrifice in the present to achieve common goals in the future, the eventual outcome of economic difficulties may be a stronger island economy, better equipped for future economic challenges. On the other hand, false prosperity based on immediate consumerism and lack of concern with the future outcome of this behavior will make the islanders flabby.

As I have said, a trade deficit cannot continue for very long time – well, not unless the island is the USA and the mainland is mainland China. For the last 35 years these two giant countries have implemented an economic policy of trade deficit, whereby the US has been importing Chinese products and China for some mysterious reason has been giving the US loans to enable it to finance these imports. But suddenly after 30 years (with the collapse of the Lehman Brothers Bank - and don't ask me what the connection is between these two events), the Chinese mainland discovered that the accumulated USA debt to China was more than one trillion US dollars (it looks like this, 1,000,000,000,000 US Dollars), which means much more than could ever be repaid, since to repay the debt the US would have to be able to export products to China, or create investment opportunities for the Chinese creditor in the USA to the same value as all the products purchased by the USA from China using those loans.

Another feature of the Chinese-US economic relationship is that over the last 35 years the rate of saving among US citizens has declined right into negative figures. This means they have had to take loans to finance their consumption. Who gave them the loans for it? If you think it was the US banks, you are mistaken. The answer is the industrious Chinese people, who have been saving almost 50% of their income, even if their per capita income is tiny compared to the average income of US citizens.

As in the case of our island economy where the fishermen forgot their fishing skills, in the case of the US too production capacity has been damaged. If you don't believe me, go and check the trend in the number of US industrial employees over the last 35 years. And if you are too lazy to do that, just recall what happened to the US car industry, which suddenly collapsed when it had to compete with its Japanese, Korean or German rivals. Just to remind you, fifty years ago, the Japanese (another big creditor of the US), the Koreans and the Chinese had no car industry at all. The US subsequently reduced its merchandise production, and instead increased its services production, mainly the financial services sector.

In the last 35 years the Chinese economy has focused on the production of gadgets to fill the US malls, supermarkets, hypermarkets, global markets, you name it. If there were a sudden depreciation of the US dollar against the Chinese Yuan, the Chinese-made gadgets would become more expensive, and there would be no buyers for all these "Made in China" products at the volume currently produced. These gadgets can hardly just be re-channeled to the Chinese market, since the Chinese have different consumer preferences. If you ever visited China you would see that every second shop is selling rice bowls, chopsticks, tea cups, tea leaves, tea or firecrackers. The Chinese taste runs to very different Products from that of US consumers, as you can see in the picture of a tee shop taken in mainland China.

After 35 years there is no easy answer to the problem of trade imbalance for either China or the USA. If China stops giving new loans to USA, the US dollar will lose its value against the Chinese Yuan. Then not only will the made-in-China products become more expensive, but the loans China has given the USA in the last 35 years will lose their value. The Chinese government may have difficulty coming to terms with the idea that the hard-working Chinese people have labored in the last 35 years mainly to make gadgets to put under the Christmas trees of American families, instead of producing products to satisfy the needs of the Chinese population. Any change in this policy would create a need to convert the production lines from Christmas gadgets to products more suitable for the Chinese market. It is not an easy task, and may take some time even for the efficient, dedicated, and hundred-percent committed Chinese workers.

As for the US government, it has its own dilemma. What is the government going to say to the domestic public if suddenly all the gadget gifts they used to buy for Christmas for 100 dollars now cost 200 dollars, and how will they persuade the car industry workers to return to their tough work of assembling cars, when they have got used to earning money in much easier and much more profitable occupations, like selling subprime mortgages. And where will they find all those middle-level managers and engineers, who in the meantime have forgotten how to produce cars, TV sets and other consumer products?

As if all this were not enough, USA, once the number-one economy of the world, will probably very soon discover it no longer enjoys that status. The conclusion is that this predicament has to come to an end very soon, and the Chinese government will have to try to recycle the money it has accumulated from the surplus with USA into the world economy instead of putting it into the vaults of the US Central Bank. This will happen partly by increasing wages and with it the standard of living of the Chinese population, so the Chinese people can buy more rice bowls, tea pots, but also cars and other merchandize that the people of USA are already fed up with, and use only because they can't figure out how to live without them.

But now let's go back to the Island, where the local economists have concluded that it is not a good thing to make sudden changes in economic realities that will change price relations with the surrounding world too fast to enable producers of the Products to adapt to those changes. It is much wiser to make gradual changes, to prevent sudden and deep distortion caused by imbalance between markets that were previously disconnected and then suddenly connected. The economists suggest that various different tools be used, ideally every tool to hand, using all of them a little rather than just one, like devaluation, too much. Their proposal is therefore a small devaluation, but also the application of import tariffs, import quotas, export subsidies etc. Most of these instruments need a government, but luckily we have not yet saddled the island with such a thing. So let us assume that the economists are successful in persuading the whole population to accept these measures because the alternative would be degradation of wages and profits, which would bring other imbalances into the island's economy. Ultimately prices will have to be adapted to the mainland prices. Of course people don't like it, but since there is no government there is nobody to be blamed for their misfortune (there are no Jews on the island). In the end there is no alternative but to balance the island economy with the mainland economy.

Yet let us suppose for a moment that mistakes made by the economists, or dissensions among the islanders, prevent any agreement being reached on economic policy. The economic problems of the island are not solved, and out of confusion and loss of self-confidence the islanders look for a strong personality to show them the right way out of the quandary. Let us say that the islanders turn to Mr. Ninel, who is famous among the islanders for coming up with clear and sharp-edged solutions whenever asked to solve any problem.

When asked what to do, Mr. Ninel immediately responds in his typical revolutionary way. Without hesitation he proposes the creation of a committee of wise men, called "The Revolutionary Wise Leadership Committee", or RWLC, and humbly accepts the nomination to be head of this committee. The very first decision of the RWLC is to destroy the bridge and the ports. Then the committee decides to implement a system of government based on a recently published new scientific theory of economics and politics, which Mr. Ninel learned about at the mainland university and which he wishes to put into practice as a socio-economic experiment.

Mr. Ninel, being famous for the resolute nature of his views, declares in front of all the islanders that this new economic governance is not just the best but the only way to solve the island's economic problem. Then quietly, and just for the ears of his closest acquaintances, he whispers that anybody opposing the new theory will have to be transferred to another much smaller island faraway in the middle of the ocean.

The closing of the ports and the bridge helps the fisherman to continue to sell their fish in the island to the islanders, but it damages the net weavers, who before the bridge was destroyed could still sell some of their products to the mainlanders. The weavers start to complain that not only have they lost their market for their nets, but they also have to pay twice as much for fish.

The RWLC decides to "islandize" all the boats, all the nets and all the net weaving machines, and to start paying all the fishermen and all the weavers the same wage. The fisherman and the net weavers will continue to fish and weave, but their products will now be centrally purchased by the RWLC and sold back through the Super-Hyper-Market chain that RWLC recently "successfully" introduced to the island.

At the beginning it looks fair that everybody will be paid the same, for after all everybody has the same stomach even if not everybody has the same capacity to produce, and the system intentionally does not reward anyone for producing more and in better quality. But the result is that slowly the amount and the quality of the products production decreases and the only way the RWCL knows how to increase the Production is to threaten the islanders who fail to fulfill the planned production quotas by accusing them of being saboteurs, which is a crime punished by long deportation to the faraway island in the ocean.

After a while the fish collectors, chosen carefully by the RWLC officers (on the basis of the right curriculum vitae including the right kind of family, meaning fishermen and not net weavers) start slacking and forget to collect the fish early at the morning. Instead they do it at noon, and by the time the fish reaches the RWLCs Super-Hyper-Market chain it has started to have an odor that the population has never smelled before, but very soon they will be used to it.

Still, the RWLC decides to create a supervisory committee to find out what the problem is with the fish supply. The committee findings clearly show that the fishermen blame the net weavers, while the net weavers blame the fishermen.

In the end the committee proposes the creation of a Five-Year Production Plan, and a statistical office to oversee its fulfillment. As the years pass, product production grows statistically but the volume of Products seems to disappear from the shelves of the RWLC Super-Hyper-Market chain. And slowly the net weavers start complaining again, and as the years go by, so do their sons and grandsons, who have never stopped grumbling about the smells in the RWLC Super-Hyper-Markets.

The arrogant net weavers go even further in annoying the RWLC committee members. Unjustly of course, since "everybody" on the island knows what hardworking people the committee members are. Just imagine the effort it takes to make the whole island economy work properly, creating 5-year plans, managing the supervision committees, gathering statistics, preventing infiltrators from the mainland getting onto the island, preventing islanders from using their boats to transfer some of the treacherous net weavers or their descendants to the mainland, and explaining to the population of the island how lucky they are that they don't live on the mainland! After all, on the mainland everybody is unemployed, famine is chronic and probably all the islanders, who had ever been foolish enough to move there, would be dead of starvation by now.

After 80 years, however, some of the islanders start to realize that probably it isn't as bad on the mainland as the revolutionary leaders claim, and maybe there might even be something in the rumors brought back by fishermen who happened to have drifted with their boats across the bay to the mainland and come back. And even the revolutionary leaders, who are not really revolutionary and not really leaders any more, since they are the third - and fourth-generation descendants of the original revolutionary leaders, start to have their doubts about the result of the socio-economic experiment. Slowly but surely realize that closing the ports and bridge brought mainly economic degradation, without any material reward. Eventually, tired of all the misery the population of the island has to go through, including sending more and more people to the smaller island in the middle of the ocean, the leaders give up and reopen the ports and the bridge.

The first time the islanders cross the bridge out of curiosity, they are utterly dazzled by all the markets and shops full of merchandise they never even knew existed; it is all so plentiful, colorful and with an attractive smell unlike that of the repulsive Super -Hyper-Market chain at "home". They feel as if they have not so much crossed a bridge to the mainland as landed on a different planet. The most amazing things of all are the shining cube-like huge buildings, much bigger than the headquarters of the revolutionary leaders committee building, and bigger even than the People's Congress hall of Culture, where out of respect no culture and no ordinary people have ever been allowed in, but only the revolutionary committee for their annual meetings.

It is not just in scale that these cube-like massive buildings are so very different from anything the islanders have ever experienced. Hundreds if not thousands of people are walking around in these buildings, apparently to enjoy leisure. They enter and exit hundreds of shops of different sizes, which offer them millions of different products, which sometimes seem to be the same, but cannot really be the same because they have different names and are wrapped in differently colored paper with different pictures and symbols. None of the products is wrapped in the thick grey-brownish paper used by the island's RWLC Super-Hyper-Market merchants to wrap their merchandise whenever they are lucky enough to have any in stock.

If all this were not enough, in the middle of the mall (which is what this wonderful building is called) there is a fountain, like one in the middle of the town square, where two pretty young girls are standing in beautiful folk costume and with wide smiles offering passers-by small pieces of different kinds of cheese, speared on toothpicks and accompanied by wine in small plastic cups... without charging even a penny for it. At first the astonished islanders are too shy to try the different kinds of cheese pieces and different tasting wines, but then one gets over his timidity and has a taste, and tries every different kind and then asks for a second turn. Surprisingly the beautiful young girls are happy to oblige. After this, all the other islanders who have been watching their courageous colleague feel confident enough to try too, and very soon a long queue of islanders is standing in front of the girls' sample counter (after all, the islanders are used to standing in queues for food).

This cheese and wine tasting comes just in time for the islanders, since they have already realized - the very first time they sat down for a rest and a cup of coffee - that what the old man used to tell them about the strength of their sterling against the dollar was very far from accurate. They have immediately done their sums and grasped that they can't afford to pay for the food, which seems to mock them with its tempting colors and aromas, as do the shopkeepers, who offer them all this merchandise in every corner of the mall, but at prices far beyond their means.

After a whole day in the mall, the islanders feel exhausted by all this plenty, overwhelmed by all these unfamiliar products, and wearied by all these smiling shopkeepers. In the evening, as they return to their island, full of emotions and questions, they start to understand that what the bridge has opened up to them is not simply the mainland just beyond the horizon, but an entirely different world.

After more visits, when their eyes start to get used to the plenty, and slowly they even begin to recognize which product is comparable to which product they used to purchase in the island, they realize that adaptation to the life of the mainland is not just a technical issue of reopening the bridge and the ports, but demands a complete transformation of values and life perspective.

At first, impressed by the clothing the mainlanders wear, the cars they ride, their sometimes rather loud, almost arrogant but free manners, the islanders regard them with humility and admiration.

Yet slowly as they get to know them better, they begin to realize that on most intellectual, practical and even emotional subjects the mainlanders are rather dull. The mainlanders show no desire to penetrate into the depth of almost any problem. Their friendships have never had to go through any affirmation by act of self-sacrifice, and they seem not to believe in values, not even in real friendship.

They are also incapable of solving almost any practical problem for themselves. Some of them can't change the flat tire in their car and have to ask a mechanic to come to do it. If a Product is broken, they don't try to fix it but just throw it away and buy a new one. They can't even repair their own bicycle, not to speak of their car. If their television set stops working, they simply buy a new one and chuck out the old one. The plastic bags are so abundant that they don't try to keep them but put them straight in the trash after using them once. And all those beautiful colorful wrappings of the products? They just tear them and toss them in the bin.

It will take ten more years for the islanders to come to understand the mainlanders better. During these ten years the older islanders will increasingly feel disappointed by the mainlanders, and distance themselves from them. Since they have no means to participate in this orgy of waste, they also start to despise the mainlanders' norms and mainly their shopping habits.

After a while they start to criticize the "mainlander character" as too focused on the material side of the life, as not concerned with fulfilling real needs but with trying to satisfy some kind of new cult based on desire to purchase, and not even to purchase a product but just the packaging of the product, although they immediately throw that away after purchase. Even if the islanders themselves enjoy using the mainland products, many of them will realize that they can't adapt their way of life, and will retreat into nostalgic memories of the good old times when people knew what was really valuable and what was not.

5. And what about a government?

No state, not even a small island state, can exist without a government. Or at least that is what the politicians like to tell to us. So the islanders decide to create a government. Now they have to cope with an entirely new question: how to form a government and what form of management system to use to govern the island? As I said earlier, our island nation is without the burden of history, beliefs, stories of kings, wars, heroes, enemies, friends, supportive friends or friends dependent on the islanders' support, and they have no distinctive culture and not even a national language. As a consequence, the island's new government will have only one task: to make the economy run as well as possible. And this means to create conditions to enable the economy to produce the maximum amount of products (do not forget that products consist of both merchandise and services), and distribute them as widely as possibly among the population without causing distortions that could slow down the process of product production.

Rather bewildered over what it means to create a government and what kind of government should be chosen, the islanders turn for advice to the oldest and the wisest man of the island, who is rumored to have studied economic and political science on the mainland in his youth.

And the wise old man said:

The very first question to ask about government is where its authority comes from;

Government often derives its authority from traditions, customs or religion, which the people feel a duty to obey, or else from force and conquest. If a government wants to derive its authority from general public support, its basic policy must be to defend the self-evident natural rights of every individual on the island, like freedom, material wealth, prosperity and well-being.

Of course there are governments that consider their purpose to be different, for example to forge a strong nation, or a state that will fulfill values believed to be higher than simply supplying the needs and wishes of individual islanders. But no higher values of this kind have been proclaimed or ever existed on this island of ours, and so the island's government will have to focus on practical issues, like economics, general welfare, security and so on. Such a government has to serve the needs of the people by creating a social contract with them, which will be approved by the islanders or/and their representatives, and written down in their books of laws. These laws will oblige the government to provide for those of the islanders' needs that cannot be met by purely individual efforts. These include services like security, support for the weakest, the old, the sick and the disabled, education for all and health for all. The main task of such a government is to create a government system that will most effectively achieve the very best results in these fields for most of the islanders.

Every government acts within a legal framework and is empowered to enforce laws over the island, its people, and its assets. It is the government's duty to punish those who violate the laws."

The old man waited for the islanders to digest all this, and then continued, "Questions of how to create a government and what kind of government will fulfill these tasks most efficiently are political rather than economic questions".

"What do you mean by political questions?" asked the islanders, and he answered;

"Political questions are questions such as, "Who is in charge? How is he chosen? Who can remove him, if at all? Who appoints him? From where does he derive his authority? Who controls him, if at all? With whom does he share political power?"

There are two very different basic solutions to these political questions, and you will have to choose between them. One is a system in which authority is diffused, which is broadly known as a democratic system, and the other is a centralized authority system called dictatorship. In dictatorship, although the government makes all the decisions it takes no real responsibility for the failures these decisions cause, and never pays the price for them, but instead blames others. By contrast, in a democracy the government can be punished by not being re-elected. Both governmental systems seek to allocate resources between sections of society, and from use today to use in the future, in the most effective and optimal way according to needs defined by them. But similarities between these two government management systems mostly end here.

Dictatorship is a political system based on the monopolization of political power, with all decision-making authority concentrated in the hands of one ruler or a committee of rulers. If dictatorship is chosen as the government system, the answers to the political questions mentioned above will probably be as follows;

a. Who is in charge? A king or dictator, or a dictatorship (where the ruler is not one person but a committee of people).

b. How is he chosen? He is self-chosen.

c. Who can remove him if at all? Nobody can remove him but the small group of his closest associates, whose fortunes and life prospects are closely connected to the destiny of the dictator or dictatorship.

d. Who nominates him formally? Usually he nominates himself, although there can be cases in which initially he is elected, but then by taking control of the military and police power he acquires all decision-making authority.

e. From where does he derive his authority? His real authority comes from his ability to threaten the population with the armed forces of the police and the military, whose loyalty he has gained by some means or other. In a dictatorship the ruler or ruling clique will nevertheless claim that their authority is derived directly from the people, but the dictatorship will never put this claim to the test by real elections, since it never sincerely asks the people for their opinion. Sometimes dictators claim that their authority is divine in origin, or that they are destined to rule, or that their authority is derived from "scientific" historical determinism. Some dictators present themselves as the personification of the people's destiny. Some of these dictators even start to believe their own claims, and will impose their authority without hesitation and without remorse. This kind of belief usually becomes stronger with time, as the dictatorship becomes entrenched and the dictator tightens his grip on power.

f. Who controls him if at all? Of course nobody controls him; in practice he tries to control everybody else.

g. With whom does he share political power? He shares political power with his closest associates, whom he chooses personally. Just as he can nominate them, he can also remove them from their positions at will. He strives to create mutual fear and distrust among his closest associates, and interprets any hint of independent meetings among them as conspiracy against his leadership. This is why his closest associates will always be the most fearful as well as the most feared people on the island. They will feel constantly threatened by those who are not in the inner leadership circle, because they are aware of the injustice and crimes they have committed against them, and they will also be afraid of their closest colleagues in the inner circle of the leadership. Most of all, they will be afraid of having any association with their colleagues without the direct involvement of the dictator himself, and of the consequences if the dictator suspects them of any dissent or conspiracy.

Dictatorships can be very effective and successful in their early stages. Dictators are good at annihilating opponents and opposition, and so are able to take and push through decisions that would create obvious advantage for the islanders but have not been taken in the past because of the competing interests of different sectors of the political spectrum. When it comes to removing from key positions people who for sectional reasons rather than the common good block obviously needed decisions, a dictator can act resolutely and without too much hesitation.

A dictator can also easily resolve situations in which a collective leadership is unable to agree on an obvious solution because of extreme differences of opinions and stubbornness. After all, the dictator can solve the problem by annihilating the fractious parties. Indeed, when he does this it may at first seem to the public that the dictator has restored "ORDER".

The political power of dictatorship is based on a network of agents whose loyalty is bought on each level of the political and administrative system by corruption. One tool of corruption is to provide them with economic rewards that are relatively small but still put them economically above the ordinary islanders. The main tool of corruption, however, is the overwhelming authority over other people's lives that these agents of the state are granted. The dictatorship allows the recruited loyalists to abuse their authority, because it believes that this practice of positioning them above other people serves the stability of dictatorial rule. This means that corruption is integral to the structure of dictatorship. Even if legally political corruption is regarded as a crime, unofficially it is accepted and a blind eye is turned because it is the building block of the dictatorial political system.

The trouble is that the political corruption of the representatives of the government will necessarily bring the economy and the society into deadlock, and reduce the government's capacity to find efficient solutions to problems as they pile up. By contrast, although corruption of political elites is also very common in democracies, there it is not only illegal on paper but cases of corruption are quite often actually prosecuted and punished with the periodic change of elected government. Even if when a dictatorship was established it was based on ideology and strong faith in the righteousness and efficiency of the economic system created by the dictatorship, the corruption built into the system of governance will inevitably have a negative effect on the economic performance of the island. The reduced economic efficiency is not just the result of the isolation of the island's economy from the mainland (which was described in the last chapter, and which a dictator may impose), but because a dictatorial political system has difficulty coping with criticism and admitting its failures, and this prevents it from making corrections to its economic policy. The economic policies of dictatorships are often based on economic dogmas that are hard to change. Since there is no actual mechanism for changing the leaders of the dictatorship, and the dictators are afraid that any change in economic paradigms could be interpreted by the public as acknowledgment of mistakes, they tend not to change their economic policies. This economic conservatism, together with the systemic corruption and lack of honest feedback from the public about the real performance of the economy, will inevitably cause problems to accumulate and the efficiency of the economy to decline.

In the modern age, dictators have had several common characteristics. They usually come to power in turbulent times of economic and political chaos, when too many individuals feel a loss of the shared practices, values and goals that previously held society together. This confusion may be caused by a lost war, deep economic dysfunction, demographic imbalances caused by mass immigration or emigration, or disproportionate internal growth of wealth of one segment of the society while the majority becomes impoverished.

When a dictator is appointed, or simply grabs political power, he does it for life, and apart from waiting for his natural death the only way to remove him is by assassination or revolution. The dictator sets himself above the laws he makes, and by doing so commits crimes against the people he is supposed to serve as their leader. A dictator typically divides the nation into two sections:

The first consists of the ordinary citizens, who will be strictly controlled. The second sector consists of a relatively small group, or army of state agents, whom the dictatorship also sets above the law and whose only function is to control the others.

This army of agent is carefully chosen from among the most desperate levels of society, who feel they have been neglected by the previous regime and ruling elites, and who have no strong connection to the other segments of the society, not even to their own families. These chosen islanders are sometimes even raised intentionally in orphanages created especially for the purpose. They are the Janissaries of the modern world. These agents are given the status of immunity to the law of the island so long as they do not act against the dictatorship itself.

Their immunity, together with their continuous criminal acts against the ordinary population, necessarily makes them a community separate from the rest of the population, which feels a common enmity towards them. Because they are trained to be alert to the actions and even the feelings of the ordinary islanders, they are aware of the fear and animosity that they inspire among the ordinary people. This position of being chosen gives them a sense of importance, uniqueness, and membership of a special elite dependent on and loyal to the dictatorship. They know very well that those who oppose the dictatorship and want to fight it are also their personal enemies, and may threaten the very existence of their sub-society, and even their lives.

These chosen agents are well aware of the daily realities of the ordinary islanders, since it is their duty to inspect and monitor them on a daily basis. Even if they do not always agree with the actions and policies of the dictatorship, their training and the fact that they are constantly scrutinized themselves mean that they will repress any feeling of remorse towards the ordinary islanders. To summarize: The personal benefits they receive from the dictatorship, which makes them materially better off than the ordinary citizens, their position of legal impunity, their power to subordinate ordinary islanders, and their feeling of belonging to an elite of chosen ones, cement their loyalty to the dictatorship and the dictator himself.

This mechanism of political corruption involving power over the lives and destiny of other people, is the core of the dictatorship and absolutely integral to it. From time to time the dictatorship may initiate well publicized prosecutions for corruption, and severely punish a "criminal", who is represented as the enemy of the system. But all this is just a show. Usually the "corrupt functionary", in fact a scapegoat, is carefully selected to ensure that the islanders are unlikely to identify with him and he is relatively easy to dehumanize. Perhaps he will be one of the merchants who were the first to profit from the economic or political confusion caused by sudden change in some basic life realities, like building bridges or closing them. If such a merchant belongs to an odd ethnic or religious group, then so much the better.

The agents of a dictatorship operate in organizations with names that are never real words, but sound more like dehumanized symbols such as KGB, SAVAK, SAVAMA, Stasi, Gestapo... Whatever their precise meaning, soon enough they become frightening icons of evil, oppression and injustice.

This technique of deforming the meaning of the words is part of the system created by dictators to create confusion, fear and submission in the hearts of ordinary citizens, who are indoctrinated to feel piety and love towards the dictator himself. If something in the politics and economy fails to work as it was supposed to according to the plans and promises of the dictatorship, the ordinary people will not be able to distinguish between the reality and the words describing these realities, which lost their true meanings as they were implanted in everyday vocabulary.

Many of the islanders will feel fear and respect for the dictator to the extent that they suppress their own selves and identify with their "leader". They will grow the same moustache as their leader, wear similar clothing, use the same phrases in conversations, and of course adopt the new meanings of words. They will say, "friendship and personal contacts are subversion", or "the expression of individuality is nihilism" and betrayal of a relative to the authorities will be called "heroism". Their support for authoritarian government will be called a "revolutionary act", and their hatred of the mainlanders "patriotism".

Some dictators are not satisfied even by near complete control of the actions of the islanders, and so try to control their thoughts as well. This they do by manipulating the islanders' instinct for self-preservation, playing on it continuously with every means at their disposal. These rulers impose their authority by inspiring fear among their closest associates, who then transmit this fear to their subordinates, and so on down to the last islander. This system creates caution and anxiety beyond imagination.

For years the dictatorship continues to rule, seemingly as indestructible as a mountain. Yet in the end the laws of nature subdue even the greatest dictator. When he finally dies, many islanders will feel as if a part of their own self died with him. So don't be surprised to see people crying at the death of the "Supreme Leader". It is not necessarily out of fear and hypocrisy. After all, only very few have the moral strength to resist such a dictatorship, and they have to be very careful, because if discovered they are immediately annihilated.

This system of falsehood, distrust and corruption is not confined to strictly political activities. It inevitably penetrates every corner of life, and above all the economy. Economic corruption is part of dictatorship, and increases over time, thus inevitably getting the economic system into major difficulties. Even so, the corruption will not be dealt with, but merely masked by a series of strategies of deception in which the dictatorship will show a great deal of ingenuity. To mention just a few: censorship, control of information flow, and bestowing favors on some specially chosen people who are well known and popular among the islanders. These selected popular islanders are either from the inner circle of the dictatorship's favorites and agents, or they are artists or sports stars whose political naivety and competitive nature mean that they are relatively easily recruited to serve the purposes of the dictatorship.

One prime example of the tools used by dictatorship to ensure its grip on power and mask its failures is control of the flow of information. Essentially it creates a mass of rules and regulations to prevent the normal circulation of information. I remember my surprise at one such regulation when I first visited Czechoslovakia just a few months after the Velvet Revolution. The Communist dictatorship had been overthrown but the old rules still persisted, as I found when I wanted to make photocopies of some documents I needed for my work. Asking where I could find a copy machine, I was told that in the city there was only one place with a copy machine for the public (I must add that this was the capital of Slovakia not a small town).

I went to the shop, where I found a middle-aged lady guarding one photocopy machine. I asked if I could copy some documents and she said, "Yes, but first you have to give me your passport". She took it and copied all my personal data by hand into a note book, and then took the pages I wanted to copy and wrote a brief description of the contents of each page in very fine hand-writing (probably the only competence she needed to perform her job perfectly), into an A4 black hard-covered notebook, which looked like the sort used by notaries to verify signatures (computers were also tightly controlled by the dictatorship). The process took several minutes, and when she had finished she went to the copy machine to copy the document by herself. I had to admit that in view of the service and all the attention I received, the price was very reasonable; it was much less than the prices in the copy centers that were to spring up like mushrooms within a few months all over the town out of nowhere, with the most modern copying equipment, where anybody could copy as much as he wanted and whatever he wanted without the need to be registered. But by that stage there was much less need to copy, since the dictatorship controls on publication had also been lifted and it was easier and cheaper for me to purchase most of the stuff I wanted to copy in the bookstores.

Ultimately none of this can stop reality percolating through the "impenetrable" borders. Even if a dictatorship seems to be strong and stable from outside, its internal unseen cracks are constantly widening, until it falls apart uncontrollably and chaotically.

Here I cannot resist mentioning a scene from a very low-quality film documentary (if you are not interested in the whole film, start it from 13 minutes in), where Saddam Hussein, standing on a podium with a cigar (probably Cuban) in his mouth, in front of his closest associates from the Baath party, reads out one by one the names of those he has decided to have arrested and killed. At each name, its owner jumps to his feet to recite verses of praise, glory, love and admiration for Saddam Hussein, until the security guards walk up to him and drag him out of the hall directly to execution. The remaining party comrades start to chant words of admiration and love, transfixed with terrified anticipation of who will be the next.

http://www.youtube.com/watch?v=fAvdYJKEdw8

When all this is over, those survivors will be the most loyal followers of the Dictator.

Modern dictatorships are more effective and ruthless than their ancient predecessors in their policy of evil, because they can make use of modern techniques of information -gathering and mass murder and withhold those techniques from the general population. Only recently, has the diffusion of information technology started to make this more difficult.

Sometimes dictators start to believe in their own divinity, or their connection to divinity. Sometimes they call the divinity GOD, sometimes destiny, sometimes historical determinism, but all of them express the leader's strong belief in his personal link to something above ordinary human existence, something eternal and even mystical, even if dressed up as pseudo - science. These dictators or dictatorships then try to change reality in line with their visions. They make cults of their own personalities, and demonize their enemies, imaginary or real. If the dictator is the leader of an island, the mainlanders are a very good candidate for demonization, and in order to prevent news of realities about the mainlanders getting through to the island he creates "impenetrable borders" to prevent infiltrators getting in as well as fugitives getting out.

These rulers are not always interested in the subject of economy in itself, but only as a tool to strengthen their authority on the population. If their beliefs happen to include some economic "doctrines", they will impose the corresponding economic dogmas zealously. These dogmas will be resistant to any evidence of reality. The whole economic system will be enslaved to the ideology and normative truth will be derived from these dogmas. The official perception of reality, based on perfectly constructed concepts and predefined truth, is above any criticism. This results in an economic system without feedback, blocking any possibility of correcting wrong economic decisions. It becomes very difficult if not impossible to react to any change in economic circumstances that demands some correction in the economic system, and the consequence is inevitably economic dysfunction. Even so, these economic systems sometimes last for generations, despite being outdated and unable to produce the results that the government originally hoped for and expected.

When dictators die their whole systems may collapse, but sometimes, when they have successfully created a whole apparatus of subordinates who identify themselves with the economic semi-realities and dogmas, this apparatus can sustain the system for many years to come. The Soviet dictatorship survived for 80 years, and outlived one of the most murderous dictators of the human history for forty years. Even now, more than half century after his death, many among his victims miss him and his "strong leadership". I would compare this phenomenon to the love and emotional dependence of a child on a father who abuses and beats him. If this is the psychological basis for the attachment felt by loyal citizens for a dictator, then it is understandable that with the death of the leader dictatorships tend to collapse, and the previously loyal citizens discover that they were betrayed, either by the dictator himself or by his associates or followers. If a dictatorship is to survive, after the death of the dictator the elite has to act with great caution but also firmness to prevent the immediate collapse of the whole system.

Inevitably I have to ask what it is about dictatorship that people can possibly value enough to support it, despite all the evils and injustices it inflicts on them? The first explanation that springs to my mind is that the dictatorship provides citizens with some kind of stability and a feeling of security. Yes, this is a stability of injustice and evil, but in the minds of many islanders it somehow becomes a source of willing conformism and identification. Dictatorships often draw on some communal ethos, based on tradition, custom and faith, or sometimes on a new ethos created by the dictatorship itself and promoted to the islanders as something they have a duty to accept and serve. Using this ethos, the dictatorship tries to forge a strong nation, supposedly dedicated to some destiny higher than simply supplying the needs and wishes of the islanders as individuals.

The wise old man paused for breath and then continued, "Let me try to sum up. The two basic government systems, dictatorship and democracy, have the same goal in the sense that in both cases the government leadership tries to keep hold of political power. Yet a democratic government does it in a more gentle way, seeking to satisfy as large a proportion of the population as possible by supplying the maximum resources to the maximum number of people, while a dictatorship does it with ferocity and without any restraint on the exercise of its political power.

In democratic political systems there are also sometimes leaders who have dictatorial tendencies or dreams, but the pluralist system of government with its checks and balances makes it difficult for them to take control. All the same, the most important thing to remember is, "IT HAPPENED IN THE PAST AND MAY HAPPEN AGAIN ".

Then the wise old man, as if he was some kind of ancient prophet, raised his voice;

"In their hearts most people have love and altruism towards others, but some do not, and often it is the man with the strongest inclination to malevolence and the strongest lust to control other people who will ultimately win the battle for political power, because his opponents will be more hesitant, with some soft spots that will make them more vulnerable. The most vicious individual can be the most successful in the struggle for power, precisely because of his willingness to employ unlimited cruelty without hesitation or conscience. He turns his brutality first against those he considers his enemies, or disloyal, then against those who just happen to be bystanders that catch his eye, and finally against his most faithful and closest followers, because it is important to keep people on their toes so that no one should ever start thinking he is indispensable".

Dictators are ridiculously peculiar and funny creatures. But let me give you one important piece of advice...Never make fun of them! They don't like humor, especially not humor at their expense.

In contrast to dictatorship, a democratic system is one in which the decision-making authority is divided among many and the legitimacy of the leaders is based on their free election by the islanders from among many candidates. The candidates for the post of rulers compete fiercely with each other before the election and after the electors have made their decision, the winners and the losers try to cooperate. In a democracy, the most important political decisions are made not just on the basis of the opinions of the elected rulers, but with a view to consensus and compromise, with the opinions of political opponents also taken in account.

A democratic system has a fixed procedure and time schedule for changing the leadership. The public does not have to wait for leaders to die, or hope that they are removed by force, even if leaders may sometimes be removed by political maneuvering before the next elections. In a democracy everybody is equal before the law, in theory at least, and in principle the law applies to the government and its members in the same way as to any other entity on the island.

While a democratic political system with its rule of law supportive to the economy has the capacity to facilitate a higher level of economic development, a dictatorship cannot sustain an efficient economy in the long run because clientelism, nepotism and corruption are bound to overtake it.

In a democracy people are allowed to make fun of the leaders, and this ridicule is even welcomed. Not that the politicians in the democracy like to be laughed at – on the contrary – but they intuitively understand the need for publicity, and all publicity, even the negative sort, is better for re-election than being ignored altogether. And that is what matters; all the rest can be flushed away with yesterday's newspaper. If you are laughed at, at least it means you are important."

As I said at the beginning of this chapter, the new Government on the island has only one task, which is to make the economy run as well as possible, and that means to create circumstances that facilitate production of the maximum amount of products demanded by the islanders and distribute them to the maximum amount of the population as evenly as possible, without causing distortions that could slow down the process of product production.

We should not confuse the policy of creating "the maximum wealth for the maximum number of people", with the policy of "creating the maximum wealth and distributing it evenly to everyone". The latter is the policy of a different island, which isolated itself from the mainland for 80 years, and after trying to create a society with equally distributed wealth, failed and gave up (viz. the previous chapter).

So let us start to explore the economic functioning of a democratic government, and here the first question should be: who is in charge of the economy in a democracy? The answer is not as easy as in the case of dictatorship, since in a democracy political power is divided between many. This division of power is one of the principles of democratically elected government. This division means than in a democratically governed island the decision-making process takes much longer and is more tiresome. Very often the decision is ambiguous and inevitably the result of compromises. Superficially and in the short term this process may seem comparatively ineffective, but during the "prolonged" process of decision-making most of the aspects of the subject are eventually taken in consideration, and even if by zigzags, usually the government will achieve its goal.

In times of economic crisis, when rather rapid decisions are expected, a democratically elected government may have problems recruiting all the political support it needs to implement the right policy. Yet when the decision is eventually taken and implemented, the results usually match up to expectations. This is because the period of discussion and argument leading up to the decision is also used to remove potential obstacles that have been anticipated in the implementation of the policy.

After listening to all this advice, and then holding long consultations and repeated elections, the islanders finally create all the necessary political organs and are able to give concrete answers to the very first political questions we outlined before: Who is in charge? How is he chosen? Who can remove him if at all? Who appoints him? From where does he derive his authority? Who controls him, if at all? And with whom does he share political power?

Let us assume that the islanders have solved these questions to their satisfaction and so now finally turn to the question of the economy. Here I should remind you of the very first sentence of this book: "Economics is a tool that helps **allocate** and utilize every limited resource available so as to maximize benefits and utility for the community and the individual".

I have bolded the word "allocate", so you can see it easily, because after all **the main economic task of every government is the correct allocation of resources between individual islanders or between the different sectors of the society, and between the needs of today and the needs of the future.**

We have already said that the island's government has no ideology but only economic goals, and these essentially consist of ensuring the maximum of products for the maximum number of people. Of course, we are assuming that the island's population is rational, and will not expect the government to do anything else (yes, this assumption of the islanders' rationality is a very odd one, but let's credit the government with being the best judge of the mentality of the island people).

So now the very first economic question confronting the government is whether to manage the economy of the island on a centralized or decentralized basis. The question is far from merely technical. So the government sits down, and with the help of the old wise man it learns that the government can manage the island economy according to one of two principles: the Market Economy (ME) or Centrally Managed Economy (CME). Don't be confused, this C makes a massive difference.

Both a Market Economy and a Centrally Managed Economy can apparently operate in either of the political systems we described earlier (a democratic system or a dictatorship), despite the huge differences between them. At least that is what is claimed by those who support a centrally managed system. It is no accident that one of the most notorious governmental systems of modern times, created in East Germany, was called the German "Democratic" Republic.

If the island is to have a Centrally Managed Economy, its government will have to take all the economic decisions, and bear all the responsibility for the functioning of the economy. This is because with a Centrally Managed Economy, unlike with a Market Economy, the government needs to create production and investment plans for every product in order to satisfy the islanders' demand. It will have to give direct instructions to all the producers on what they will produce and how much, and on what share of the resources will be allocated from today's usage to future usage, and which projects to invest in to make optimum use of the increase of potential production capacity to provide maximum future benefit for the islanders.

If all this were not enough, the government officials, who are not always the most energetic people, will also have to decide what will be the determining factor for fixing the product price, and calculate the price of every product sold in the island accordingly. The easiest and commonest way to calculate the product price is by calculating its costs, but this pricing system is problematic in many respects. It requires yet more decisions: decisions about wages and rewards paid to those who will be involved in the production process, and the price of the raw material used for the product production. If the cost of raw material is derived only from production costs, the price will take no account of the relative scarcity of the specific raw material. This may cause depletion of the scarce raw material if it is under -priced, or distort its effective use if it is overpriced.

Since the pricing system itself is a tool for the allocation of resources, it seems to have potential as a means to achieve social and political goals. If for example the fishing-net price is too high, the fishermen will become relatively poor and the net weavers will get rich, while if it is too low, the net weavers will become poor and the fisherman rich. So the pricing of products cannot be regarded as just a technical issue, but is a major social and consequently political issue that will always involve preference to a certain section of society, for example a section traditionally more supportive of the existing government.

A different product pricing system might involve combining the two attributes of the product, i.e. the relative scarcity of the raw material and the cost of the inputs needed to produce the product. We could go on and on debating the question of how and why this system of pricing is preferable to the other one, but at all events it sounds like a huge job, and to tackle it the island government will have to create a Central Planning Committee. Let us assume that the Central Planning Committee has a supercomputer able to calculate all the prices of all the Products marketed in the island fast and without mistakes, and using any principle of price derivation decided upon.

When the Central Planning Committee is asked to solve the puzzle of product price interrelations, it will very soon discover that the relative pricing of different products is not an economic question but a political one. Since it is operating in a democratically managed government system, it turns to the elected government to decide on the most important aspect of the pricing system - which is who will earn how much. We have already said that a pricing system calculated in this way implies differentiation in rewards to different sectors of society. The Central Planning Committee, hoping to calm political opposition to their government, may decide to give preference to the net weavers, whose political preferences are against a centrally managed economic system because of the highly individualistic and competitive character of their work. In contrast, the fisherman are relatively supportive of the centrally managed government, because they are used working as a community, helping each other, and their political attitudes have always been more communal than individualistic. In these circumstances the government may decide cynically to neglect the economic interests of the fisherman, who can anyway be counted on to support the centrally managed system, and to try to buy the support of the net weavers. Or alternatively the government may take the opposite line of giving preference to the fishermen, to consolidate their support. In either case the government will fix the relative price of the nets as compared to the fish price, and the relative income of the different sectors of the society will change accordingly.

After long deliberation about all the advantages and disadvantages of different relative prices of nets to fish, the democratically elected government eventually fails to find any better solution than a compromise: it decides to fix the relative prices in such a way that both the fishermen and the net weavers will get the same income. A decision of this kind not only makes the price calculations easier, but also secures the even distribution of income. Unfortunately it is a mistake to think that the move will satisfy everyone. The net weavers consider themselves highly professionalized, and see no reason why should they get the same wages as the fisherman, who need no training and education to do their job. For their part, the fisherman are just as resentful, and ask why they should get no more than the net weavers, who don't have to get up early at the morning and risk their lives on fragile boats out in the waters of the bay. And who are those net weavers anyway? Just a nuisance to the beloved centrally managed government!

As the next step, the government of the centrally managed system will have to create a hierarchical management and functional units to channel the decisions from the top decision- maker down to the last entity active in the production process, the one that will implement the decision made by the Central Planning Committee and actually produce the Product that is transferred to the customer. If this system is to be effective, it has to create a feedback system from the markets. So the government will create a Production Market Controllers department, which will monitor the information coming from the markets about the Products, analyze the findings and submit reports to the Central Planning Committee, which will then react to the reports and make continuous changes and updates to the production plans on that basis.

Superficially the Centrally Managed Economy system looks very effective. It can concentrate the production of each product in one facility, training producers there to be the very best in their field by allowing the facility to specialize and professionalize in one specific single product. If the task of the island economy is to supply the most basic needs of the population, theoretically this specialization should ensure the most effective production results.

The islanders soon discover that the Centrally Managed Economy is indeed very effective when it comes to realization of big projects on the national level, where there is need to recruit and unify the efforts of a large part of the island population and overcome major obstacles. The very best such example is in times of war, when all the effort is concentrated on the single purpose of winning the war. Other obvious examples include huge national investment projects that are too big and too risky for a private entity, with very long-term return rates and many side-effect considerations. This kind of undertaking includes allocating economic activities to under-developed locations, investing in future technologies with uncertain outcome, or concentrating on the development of whole regions on a large scale. A Centrally Managed Economy also seems more efficient when it comes to more even distribution of wealth among the population, since it can easily switch resources from one section of island society to the others by administrative decision.

On the other hand, personal wealth is not determined by current income alone, but also includes the accumulated property owned by individual islanders. Some of this property may even be used as a tool for economic activity not directly connected to the Central Planning Committee plan. What is more, it may generate additional income for the asset owners in a way that is at odds with the plans of Central Planning Committee for the even distribution of wealth among the islanders. The Central Planning Committee will eventually have to decide to "islandize" all the privately owned assets with the potential to create economic activity and income that is not in line with its planning.

In spite of the advantages of a Centrally Managed Economy for creating specialized production capacity on a large scale, even distribution of income, and greater potential for investment in large-scale projects, it has one very big disadvantage. This is that it lacks the flexibility in decision-making so crucial in the modern age, when a new Product appears on the market every day, and disappears from it the next. Let us imagine that the first signs of mismanagement in our island economy appear when islanders start complaining about the quality of the goat cheese, with its many attributes, like fat content, color, mold culture, smell, taste, etc. It becomes more and more complicated to give the production facilities the right instructions on what precisely to produce and how much of it and of what quality. The Central Planning Committee therefore decides to create norms that will define the product quality and reduce its variability. By the way, did you know that all the confectionary producers in all the communist countries had only one recipe for each kind of cake? If you visited Sofia or Prague in communist times, you would eat exactly the same cheesecake in both cities, with no other kind available. If an adventurous cook added some raisins that were not specified in the norm for cheesecake (assuming he could get hold of any raisins), he could be accused of subversion and punished for it.

It turns out that in spite of a supercomputer and huge management efforts, the Central Planning Committee cannot correctly predict the amount of consumption of every product. Inevitably, as it keeps making mistaken predictions and so the supply fails to match the demand, the solution will be the rationing of some products and the stockpiling of others. And so we arrive at the phenomena of endless queues for Products in demand on one side, and huge storage space needed for unsold products on the other side.

This predicament is vividly illustrated by an experience I had in an Eastern Europe country in the times of economic transformation from a centrally managed to a market economy. A friend of mine, who had purchased a supermarket from the government, invited me to join him when he took possession of his new shop. We entered the shop, walked between the empty shelves, and found ourselves in front of a locked door. We had to try all the keys before finally the last one opened the door and we found ourselves in a huge storage space full of identical grey boxes piled up from the floor up to the ceiling. Wondering what treasure we had discovered, we opened one of the boxes, to reveal six perfectly wrapped smaller boxes. When we opened one of the smaller boxes, we discovered that it contained six small metal CO_2 soda chargers. People used to screw these onto bottles of still water to make the water fizzy. Do you remember this product? If not, probably you are too young to recall the 1960s and 1970s, when it was in fashion for at least 10 years.

Even in communist Eastern Europe, though, this product was replaced long ago by soda water in plastic bottles. But it seems that someone in the Central Planning Committee forgot to give orders to stop producing them. If you ask me why the centrally managed communist economy collapsed, I would say it was probably because of lousy inventory management. And I wouldn't be joking.

As I have said, in a centrally managed economy prices are administratively decided, which means that some products in great demand are underpriced. Let us take a fishing hook as an example. In a market economy, if there is a big demand for fishing hooks, the problem is solved by a price increase initiated by the supplier. On the other hand in our centrally managed island the hook prices are indexed to the costs of production, and an increase in demand does not affect the selling price.

In the market economy the hook price rises with the increased demand, while the production costs remain at their original level. The increased gap between the selling price and production costs will accumulate added value for the supplier of the hook, or in other words "DAS KAPITAL".

In a market economy, Capital (by the way, its name in the market economy is Equity, a much less highly charged term) makes it possible to allocate resources to investment in activities with greater added value and profit. In a centrally managed economy, by contrast, there is no use for capital accumulation, since the decisions on all investments and allocation of resources are made centrally and administratively. Thus any change of prices not in line with the pre-determined system based on production costs would cause disruption in the centrally managed economy. This is why the prices have to remain fixed, otherwise, if the public believes (and this is all about faith) that a product's price is lower than its real value, people will want to purchase more of the specific product (the hook). So long as the product price continues to be lower than the value subjectively associated with it by the consumer, no decision of the Central Planning Committee to increase Production quotas will solve the problem of under-supply.

What is more, the hooks will disappear from the market, and only those lucky enough to have contacts with the shop keepers selling the hooks will be able to purchase them freely. Every rumor of a new delivery of hooks will cause immediate queues in front of the Hook Stores, because the public has the feeling that hooks are a product in deficit (*) or in other words scarce, and everything scarce is valuable, even if not very useful, like diamonds for example. The pressure on the suppliers will grow until all the islanders have so many hooks that they finally realize they have more hooks than they will need for their entire life, and to make it even worse, there are many islanders who will not be using the hooks for fishing at all, but will have bought them just to own a valuable object. Exactly as some women like to own expensive diamond earrings, and when wearing them to a night ball need an escort of at least two bodyguards... So instead of wearing the diamonds, they prefer to put the real diamond earrings in a bank safe and wear glass imitations that look the same but don't need bodyguards.

The example of hooks explains the difference between the product price systems in the Centrally Managed Economy and the Market Economy. **The price in the Market Economy is decided by the subjective feelings of the islanders about the scarcity or abundance of the Product.** Sophisticated marketing experts work very hard to create a feeling of scarcity around a newly lunched Product. Apple has done it very successfully with I-Phones and I-Pads, and created long lines of fans, who sometimes even sleep in front of the I-Pad and I-Phone shop doorsteps to make sure they are among the very first to own the new Product. In a Market Economy nothing is better than consumers queuing up for a new product, not because it is scarce but because the producer has successfully created the illusion that it is scarce. On the other hand, the queuing consumers in a Centrally Managed Economy are proof of the failure of the system. In the Market Economy the scarce product is relatively expensive, while on the other hand products that are abundant are relatively cheap. Think of tee-shirts without a logo brand and tee-shirts with some stylish printing on them. It's the same product as far as use is concerned, but the price is entirely different.

(*) "Narrow Profile", were the actual words used in Czechoslovak slang for Products scarce in the shops.

Here we come back to our theory of the collapse of the centrally managed communist economy. One of the basic production management principles in the market economy is known as "Just in Time". There are professionals who claim that Japanese production efficiency owes much to this production principle.

To explain very briefly the meaning of "Just in Time": the idea is that the most efficient and cost-effective production system is when the inventory of products in production and final products is reduced to a minimum. To have a large inventory is very costly; the goods may be stolen, damaged or may deteriorate, and above all they may become outdated and unwanted, as happened to the CO2 soda chargers, but also to last season's fashion clothing. Obviously, if in storage for too long these products lose all or most their value.

According to the production strategy of "Just in Time", the absolute ideal would be that when a consumer enters the shop and orders a product, the production process starts immediately and the product is supplied exactly according to the consumer's needs, directly from the raw materials within few minutes.

Does any such product and production process exist? Definitely! The very best example of an ideal production process of this kind is a good pizzeria, where the supplier (the cook) immediately to the demand of the consumer (the waiter is just the unnecessary camouflage of the luxury), and using the raw materials (flour, water, vegetables, cheese and tomato sauce) produces within 10 minutes a meal perfectly adjusted to the demands of the consumer, who may even ask for extra pepperoni or olives if he wants. The opposite of the pizzeria in this sense is the workplace dining room, (by the way, these used to be very popular in communist countries), which offers the same menu of three courses (soup, main course and desert) every day, or in some more illustrious workplaces a regular different menu for each day of the week, repeating itself every week. If one of the workers dislikes the food and brings sandwiches made by his wife to work instead, his portion has to be thrown into the dustbin.

In a centrally managed economy the production management system is exactly the opposite of the "just in time" system. Some products are produced even if there is no demand for them, while products in high demand are stored in the houses of the consumers in their final form, waiting for the right time to be used, if ever. Sometimes the right time comes only after months or years, and sometimes it never comes. This is obviously very contrary to the ideal way of keeping inventory in the form of raw material. Interestingly, the jargon in the communist countries perfectly reflected this reality. In a communist country, if a citizen passed a queue of people who had heard rumors that this particular shop would be getting a delivery of some scarce product, he would always stop and ask them, "What are they giving out here today?". He would never ask, "What are they selling here today?" The unrealistically low price of the scarce product makes it look as if it is virtually free of charge in the eyes of the purchaser.

One time when I was visiting a communist country, I noticed queues for the most basic food products, like vegetables or meat. Talking to a local friend I asked him, "How do you survive under such conditions?" At first he looked at me with surprise and then chuckled as he opened his cupboards. They were full of home-made smoked sausages, smoked meat, pickles and jams, and then my friend showed me his refrigerator stuffed with frozen products. All this is exactly the opposite of the production system of "just in time". He kept all the final products in the most expensive long-term storage place, his home. I would add that this friend of mine, a professor of physics, used to focus his extraordinary technical skills on improving the sausage machine he had made out of empty tins.

By the way, do you remember the supermarket with the CO2, the one that my friend purchased during the economic transformation with that huge storage occupying half the shop? Within a few months he rebuilt the storage room to create additional selling space and he put all his merchandise out on the shelves of the shop. He did not need storage place at all, because there was no need to hide the product in demand under shelves for family members, friends and useful acquaintances.

Eventually the bureaucrats of the Central Planning Committee will become aware of the chronic problem they have with creating a match between supply and demand. After deep analysis they will decide that they can remedy the continuous shortages of products and long queues of islanders by changing the island population's consumer behavior. This will involve compelling the islanders to consume the products produced in line with the Central Planning Committee's Production planning.

Yet to the enormous frustration of the bureaucrats, the island population will stubbornly refuse to behave rationally. Just when the Central Planning Committee decides to produce enough grey woolen trousers for every male citizen of the island, the islanders develop a mysterious fondness for blue cotton trousers, with holes in the knees. To make the situation even more difficult, the women for whom the Central Planning Committee has planned beautifully woven red skirts suddenly decide to wear the same ugly, blue cotton worn-out pants too.

This is all too much even for the calm, moderate bureaucrats of the Central Planning Committee, and so they decide to retaliate and send the police to pick up all the blue cotton trouser wearers and send them to re-education centers, where they will be taught about aesthetics and proper behavior.

Many people blame the failure of the centrally managed economy on the mistakes of the leaders, not the system itself. After all, the centrally managed economy seems to be obviously more efficient in principle. Everybody can understand that someone has to run the economy, and its management cannot be left to some invisible, intangible market force. Obviously a centrally managed economy ought to be more efficient and successful with its policy of even distribution of wealth. If you hear these claims, do not believe them. All the faults of the centrally managed system, so evident in "communist" countries, were caused by the failure of the system itself. The problems of the centrally managed economy became ever more visible as the consumer basket became ever more diversified, changing with every new invention and every new fashion. In a modern economy nobody can fail to notice in everyday life that new innovative products keep appearing on the market and transforming existing paradigms of consumption, as happened with mobile phones. The first mobile phones weighed several kilograms and could hardly have replaced fixed phones, but then they grew smaller and even started replacing cameras, and then computers and now televisions, newspapers, books and God knows what else will come next. Let's just hope mobiles will not replace us humans.

By the way, when did you last speak on a fixed phone? There are of course rumors about damage to health caused by mobile phones. I wonder who is behind the rumors. Maybe some fixed phone line owners?

There is a famous story from the post-war period when communist governments took political power in Central Europe. The communists created a central planning office which among its other myriad tasks analyzed the nail situation in the country and came to the conclusion that one factory would be enough to supply all the nation's nail needs. So they closed all the nail factories except for one production facility in a remote underdeveloped region in the eastern part of the country. It was a perfect plan to kill two birds with one stone: to supply the nails much needed in post-war times and to increase employment in an underdeveloped region. The central planning office gathered all the necessary information, and after consideration of all the factors they presented a production plan for the next five years to the only factory producing nails (the socialist five-year plan, do you remember?). The trouble was that over the next five years nails disappeared from the market. To make new furniture the carpenters were forced to fall back on pulling the old nails out of old broken furniture. Whenever the Central Planning Committee received complaints about nails from the association of the carpenters' cooperatives, they would check the reports of the Production Market Auditors and would find that the plant was producing exactly the amount planned, and even produced more after it was urged to do so. In the next five-year plan, to be on the safe side the Central Planning Committee doubled the nail production plan, but there was still a lack of nails for carpenters. At the end of the second five-year plan a supervisory committee was sent to the nail plant. It reported that the plant had fulfilled the production plan perfectly, but had produced mainly large nails, since the plan quotas had been defined just in kilograms!

Another major aim of a government running a centrally managed economy is full employment. Yet in every society there are individuals who for one reason or another are unfitted for work or do not want to work, and if they are to be employed they have to be forced into jobs. Then there are situations when some production facility has to be closed because of the irrelevance of the product it produces, like the soda charger factory mentioned above. In such cases, if the government has taken on itself the obligation to find the workers at the soda charger plant new jobs immediately, it cannot do so on the basis of free choice but only by forced transfer of the workers from one occupation to another.

Countries with centrally managed economies tend to reduce the political and personal freedom of the population. Is this inevitable? Freedom of entrepreneurship is something that a Centrally Managed Economy definitely cannot allow, but what about the other aspects of personal freedom? Does setting limits on the freedom of economic activity of the individual necessarily entail limits on other fields of creativity? A different question might be: is the freedom of the individual more important than a more even distribution of the wealth? Is the right to personal ownership of assets generating yield, and the right of economic entities to generate capital income for the owners, necessary for the achievement of personal freedom, or is it just a tool for the defense of the economic position of the ruling economic elites?

Could a centrally managed economy coexist with the enjoyment of freedom and political rights? As far as I can see there is no logical connection between personal freedom and a market economy, nor any necessity to limit personal freedom when a centrally managed economy is applied. Yet historically the model of the centrally managed economy has been applied to solve problems of the whole community rather than the individual. This is clear from the central goal of economic equality in the centrally managed model, while the market economy model does not have economic equality as a top priority. If the aim of equality is taken to extremes, as happened in the communist countries, it has to entail limitation of personal freedom. After all, if the activities of the entrepreneurial type of person are not restricted, he will always find ways to increase his wealth at the expense of the more passive islanders. So if absolute equality is the final aim of the government, personal freedom has to be curtailed."

Here the wise old man perceiving the islanders, dissuaded from creating a centrally managed economic system, continued, "So now we should turn our attention to the decentralized economic system called Market Economy...."

The most fundamental belief underpinning the market economy is that the aim of every economic entity, from the smallest self-employed individual to the greatest international corporation, is to maximize his or its profit and wealth. For the followers of the Market Economy, profit-making is a positive phenomenon that advances not just the individual economic entity but the whole economy. Profit is the result of the added value that the entrepreneur creates by being better than the others, either by reducing his production costs or by creating better Products which attracts more consumers for higher prices. Increased profitability will lead to the accumulation of capital in the profitable enterprise and enables it to expand its successful activities. Both the reduction of costs and the improvement of the Product are associated with the excellence of the profit-making entity, in contrast to the failure of an entity that generates loss.

Here we see the very first sharp difference between a centrally managed economy and a market economy. The centrally managed system encourages and protects mediocrity in the individual, whereas the market economy encourages excellence. Another clear difference between the two is that "while the centrally managed economic system is supportive for the suppliers, the market economic system favors the consumer".

In post-communist countries I often met economically successful individuals who had become rich with the change of the economic system from a centrally managed to a market economy. They tended to complain of the envy of their less successful childhood friends, who couldn't come in terms with their success. Typically they blamed it on the local national mentality. Sincerely but in vain, I would try to explain to them that this envy has nothing to do with the national mentality. On the contrary, the envy of friends is a very general phenomenon in other places too. I even told them that envy is a major engine that drives entrepreneurs toward ever greater achievements. It is the force behind the general impulse toward excellence in the market economy society. In the end I had to give up. Nobody wanted to accept that the system of market economy, which had in a few years done so much to raise the standard of living of all the citizens of the post-Centrally Managed Economies, could be based on so "ugly" a human phenomenon as greed.

Speaking of greed, let me tell you a real story, which happened in the sixties in a kibbutz, hidden between the hills of northern Galilee in Israel. If you are not familiar with kibbutzes, at that time they were small cooperative villages with few hundred members living in communities, without any private possessions. In the kibbutz all the important decisions were made by the general assembly of the kibbutz members and applied equally to all members. The kibbutz members were not paid for their work, and all their personal needs were covered by the community. The only money they received for their work was pocket money, enough to purchase cigarettes, candies and other small stuff.

Cainele, one of the members of this kibbutz, was a great lover of classical music and had one big dream in his life - to purchase a gramophone so he could privately listen to the music he loved so much. Of course a gramophone was well beyond his financial means, but Cainele did not give up his dream, and instead gave up smoking, and coin by coin he started to save up his pocket money. After ten years self-denial of any kind of "luxury", he finally had enough to pay for the so much desired gramophone.

But just by chance, very soon after Cainele purchased the gramophone, the kibbutz started to prosper economically, and after serious consideration the managers decided to share the new "wealth" with the kibbutz members. On the principle of equality they made a proposal at the general assembly of the kibbutz that all kibbutz members should be given a brand new gramophone, exactly the kind that our music-loving acquaintance had bought a half year before. Guess who fought most fiercely against the decision?

Adopting a market economy means that the island has to provide support and freedom to everybody who sincerely wishes to produce and sell products on the markets. It has to encourage the entrepreneur's eagerness to make profits. The islanders have to adore the successful, even if out of envy. They have to be supportive, even if out of contempt for those who failed in their ventures. Another crucial principle, however, is that the market economy should be based on legality and the equality of everybody before the law. No one, not even the government, should be judged by different standards.

If an economic entity is successful, it is because it has successfully created product for which there is a demand, at a price higher than the production costs, and can produce more and more of this product until it satisfies the demand while profiting from it. The higher price of the product, which is caused by its scarcity compared to the demand, is translated into profit for the supplier.

When there is no demand for his product, a producer will stop producing it, so as not to incur losses. If a producer still insists on producing a good or service when there is no demand for it he will go bankrupt. This system not only automatically regulates the volume of the product production and supply quotas in line with demand, but also allocates resources to activities where they are most needed by the consumers. In a market economy a CO2 soda charger producer will not survive if he fails to stop his production line when consumers stop wanting his CO2 Product and start purchasing soda water in plastic bottles.

The market economy needs no Central Planning Committee and Production Market Auditors and no production quotas or pricing of the products. The producers will either do their own planning, following the market reaction and producing enough products to satisfy demand "just in time", or they will simply not be there anymore.

How do producers decide on production quotas? If over-producing, the producer will immediately suffer for his error by having the additional unnecessary costs of a pile-up of unsold products, which puts him at a disadvantage compared to his competitors. And if he doesn't produce enough there will always be someone else to replace him and push him out of the market. If the entrepreneur is not talented enough to keep in touch with the signals from the market, and to react to these signals correctly, fast, and proportionately, he will simply go out of business. The supporters of the free market economy believe that this natural mechanism is the very best economic planner and regulator.

It is also the root of many business failures caused by unexpected (but usually perpetual) external or internal changes in the economic environment. Often these unexpected changes precipitate personal tragedies as occupations become irrelevant: coachmen disappear when replaced by bus and taxi drivers, or shoe repairers vanish, no longer needed because of product standardization and the reduction of production costs.

The decision-making process in a Market Economy requires no central decision-maker. The many small competing suppliers, trying to outdo each other in the battle for consumers, are all playing the game of optimal utilization of resources.

In a Market Economy, the economic decisions are made by many separate participants in economic life, who compete fiercely out of antagonism and sometimes even out of hate. This sometimes seemingly very chaotic play, demanding continuous alertness from each participant of the game, hones the survivor instinct of the entrepreneurs. This is the driving force behind the ambition for excellence of every participant in the competitive market economy, and, as in the jungle, only the strongest survive while the weak go to the wall. And let us not forget that in the market economy the strongest player is the one with the cheapest and the most attractive Products. This is very much in contrast to politics, where the strongest is the most ruthless.

Yet this hymn of glory I have been singing to the market economy is by no means the whole story. The market system often fails to achieve perfect resource allocation. Usually it has difficulty coping with long-term problems created by the short-sightedness of the supplier- producer- marketer chain, driven by the desire for short-term profits, and of consumers driven by their lust for possession. The most telling example is the car industry, which in its keenness to sell more and more cars created a nimbus of glory around this product, transforming it from a product supplying a certain form of transportation into a product offering self-image, radiating sex-appeal, manhood, the expression of independence, and so forth. The consequences have been endless traffic jams, city streets stuffed with parked cars and excessive road networks, destroying nature and the environment. Private cars have become more a nuisance than a pleasure and more an obstacle to smooth transportation than an efficient tool for it.

One very extreme case of the malfunctioning of a market economy because dominant market players exploit their influence to their own advantage and to the detriment of general prosperity occurred in the USA. In the mid-20th century the car and oil-producing companies bought up the public traffic companies running electric trams just in order to get rid of trams altogether. They replaced the trams by petrol-fuelled-motor buses produced by themselves. This caused major change of the US cities, and not for the better.

The task of the government in a market economy is not to plan and manage but to supervise the functioning of the markets, and intervene when some discrepancy occurs.

Another necessary task of government is to diffuse the wealth among as many citizens as possible, and at least relatively evenly, without causing too much disruption in the economy. There are two rationales behind this task: first the perceived need to secure a decent livelihood for everybody, and second, the belief that redistribution of wealth is positive for the whole society and economy, and is morally right. If the government did not intervene to redistribute wealth, the market economy would consign the less fortunate and capable to despair.

A comparison between the centrally managed and the market economy naturally brings up the most common question that everybody has asked himself at least once: "what is all this life about?" "Is it an adventure in which the main point is to fight to become the very first, the very best, the most excellent in the field of your activity and knowledge, and try to conquer the world in this field, or is it about ensuring the greatest security and stability, mediocrity and routine, without any need to tackle challenges and take risks in pursuit of personal fulfillment?

People who like to be coordinated and managed by others will probably prefer the environment created by the centrally managed economy. By contrast, people who want to manage their own lives will prefer to be active in an economic environment created by the market economy. Of course, not everyone fits neatly into one category or the other. There is a spectrum from one to the other and people's positions on it probably also reflect positions on the political spectrum.

Freedom of personal choice entails personal responsibility for every decision. We should not be surprised, and still less contemptuous, that some people prefer a government imposing strict rules and demanding personal obedience over freedom of personal choice. It is common for people faced with a crucial decision to look around for advice. This search for authority, whether in the form of other people or in the idea of God, is the expression of a general need for someone with whom we can share our responsibility.

You should ask yourself if you are more the type who prefers to be managed and coordinated by others, or the type who likes to manages your own life and sometimes even the lives of others. If you can develop the ability to give yourself a truthful answer to this question, you will probably become more content with what you are, and may even become happier in your life.

Another of the centrally managed economy's attraction may be that it is relatively simple and easy to understand in principle. Everybody can grasp a system in which there is some kind of "Big Boss", who takes care of everything and manages everybody, and doesn't require anyone to do anything more difficult than simply fulfill his orders. I would say that the centrally managed economy is perfect for the more juvenile dependent people, who like to let the others to make decisions for them.

Belief in this system with a visible governor, rather than in a system governed by the invisible hand of the market, fulfills the same kind of functions as conspiracy theories, which are essentially very simple explanations of phenomena that people find apparently inexplicable or difficult to understand. To many people it is easier to believe in a mythological story based on fiction or sometimes a theory of evil, with a very clear logical structure based on an imaginary story or lie, than to make the effort to look carefully at the evidence, to verify or reject the validity of the claim.

Compared to the centrally managed economy, the unsystematic system of the market economy, full of competition, envy and sometime unfair practices, looks frightening, out of control and unpredictable. Yet surprisingly, out of chaos it creates a state of harmony and co-operation, and with it general economic well-being. This ability of the market to create harmony out of chaos reminds me of a good jazz band, where loosely defined codes, pre -agreed among the band players, allow every participant of the band to play a different instrument and a different tune while at the same time in some very odd way producing a well-orchestrated melody.

All the same, not everything in the Market Economy is perfect. The market economy is an endless struggle for survival and domination, where the most successful, the very best, becomes bigger than his competitors and the less successful are cornered and often annihilated. The most basic instinct of every entrepreneur in the market economy system is to destroy all the other players, rivals who occupy a share of the market in which he is active. Sometimes one player can become so dominant in a market that he marginalizes or drives out the others. At this point he can raise the prices of his products and sometimes neglect their quality. However this success is short-lived, for even when a business manages to destroy its closest competitor, whenever it then raises product prices to increase its profits or reduces product quality, a new competitor will soon appear offering lower prices and penetrating the market with a product more adjusted to the needs of the consumers. Of course, a strong producer-supplier often tries to annihilate the smaller ones by using unconventional methods, such as physical force, threats, and dumping prices (pricing products below the production costs). If all this were not enough, they sometimes use their economic resources to try to purchase political influence and so secure legislation that bolsters their position of dominance in their niche of the market. To prevent this disregard for fair play, the island has to create a legal system that will maintain a level playing field for every individual entrepreneur.

Another persistent source of disruption in the market economy is actually built into the legal structure of the publicly owned and traded economic entities responsible for most of the economic activity in the modern market economy. Ownership of these publicly owned and traded share companies is widely dispersed among the public. This ownership structure means that the majority of the company owners are very small share-holders, and this gives disproportionate power to a few dominant share holders, who even if they hold a minority share of corporation stakes, still have full control of the publicly owned company.

Externally nominated managers of investment or pension funds hold large stakes of shares in public share companies. This gives these managers decisive authority in the public share companies whose shares their funds possess. The real owners of the pension funds are again the common people, who have saved some part of their income to secure themselves for their old age. Most of the depositors in these funds are private employees depositing their savings in commercial bank, small investors entrusting their savings to an investment fund, or savers in life insurance or pension funds. All these small lifelong savings are entrusted into the hands of "professionals", who invest them in publicly traded share companies. These managers of investment funds, insurance companies, banks, etc. (the so-called financial institutions), as representatives of these investment and pension funds, are appointed to directorships of the publicly owned companies, and so control and nominate the executive management of these companies.

The trouble is that the publicly owned share companies are usually also the biggest clients of the financial institutions, and as such they are nominated to become directors of the financial institutions themselves. And here we see the genesis of a closed circle of managers, who nominate each other, and can advance their own personal self-interest rather than the interest of the owners of the entities they supposedly represent. The problem arises from the vagueness of the connection between share ownership and public share company management.

In principle, the public share companies' managers are subject to supervision and checks by well - established audit firms, which are supposed to be guardians of the interests of the shareholders. Yet again the auditors are recruited and paid by the managers of the companies they are supposed to audit. This makes them liable to be influenced by a consumer-supplier relationship with those managers. The scandalous case of Enron and its auditors Arthur Anderson is a well-known example of the failure of the audit control system to protect the interests of ordinary share-owners in a publicly traded company as a result..

This kind of distortion is very hard to prevent in the capitalist system, because the whole system is driven by competitiveness and the general desire of every individual for ever increasing wealth. Contrary to the assumptions behind the system, the instruments used to achieve this goal are not always beneficial for the economy and the general public. In some cases the legal system seems to have difficulty coping with misuse of the system for personal gain at the expense of the general public and the rightful owners.

The role of government policy in the market economy should be to supervise and help to secure the functional operation of the markets, and to intervene when some discrepancy occurs. It has to make laws that support private entrepreneurship and apply equally to every islander, and it has to have a core commitment to personal freedom and the sacredness of private property. The basic belief behind the market economy is that implementation of agreed rules securing an stable economic environment where every economically active person will act in his own best interest will ensure that the market is supplied with the cheapest and the best products most in demand with consumers. In other words all parties involved (the government, the entrepreneurs, the financial sector, the suppliers, etc.) will act according the rules of fair play.

The market economy system is more effective in achieving maximum utilization of resources where flexibility in decision-making is needed.

Decision-making is spread among many small units, and is not concentrated in bureaucratic hierarchical management systems, which have a tendency to grow rampantly, become tangled, and ultimately fossilize. If the economy needs to produce a wide range of different products that are changing fast and continually, it needs very dynamic decision making, which is just what centrally managed economies have failed to provide.

The market economy can be characterized as a system that emerges from the spontaneous chaotic behavior of each individual economically active entity, with all entities being driven by the general aspiration for profit and hegemony. In actual fact, not everybody has this drive to profit and hegemony, and this is a good thing because if they did then chaos could overwhelm the whole system. With their drive for profit and hegemony, the very few very best entrepreneurs will eventually become economic leaders, who cut a path for all the others and pull them forwards.

Olympic competitors work very hard on self-improvement, trying to reach a godlike perfection, and achieving a new record only spurs them to do even better. But only a very few sportsman compete in the Olympics, and finally only one wins the most precious prize of being the very best and enjoying the glory and sometimes a moment of personal satisfaction. The risks, the discomfort, the need for total commitment and so on, are all part of the price paid for the achievement of becoming the very first. The same is true of the foremost entrepreneurs. These economic leaders keep trying to reach new heights, with new inventive initiatives, in many fields of economic activity. It might be the invention of a new product, but it could also be a new understanding of some change in the economic environment, or just a wish to enlarge existing activity within a routine already successfully tried many times. All their efforts are focused on the goal of being the very first, the ultimate winners.

The most successful players in the market economy are the super-entrepreneurs, who not only start a new business activity from scratch, but introduce onto the market entirely new products that prove to be so popular that consumers wonder how they could ever have existed without them. This kind of product entrepreneurialism reaps the highest rewards. If you wonder which products are of this kind, just look around you and work out which of the products you now use on a daily basis did not exist even as concepts ten to twenty years ago. You will be surprised how dependent you are on these products.

I would like to offer a few examples, like the mobile phone, but also the Internet, television and before that the automobile. As cars became available to all, they gave rise to suburbs and outlet malls, but also traffic jams, parking lots, and a huge road network. Television brought change in the pop culture, the Internet brought democratization of human creativity in the fields of entrepreneurship, culture, consumerism and so forth. Finally the mobile phone has revolutionized work possibilities and social life. I could mention many other technological breakthroughs that have changed the paradigms of human behavior in the last hundred and fifty years, but you probably have the idea by now.

Another aspect of the radical difference between the economic systems of Centrally Managed and Market Economy is the difficulty of the transformation of one into the other. Throughout history such transition has always involved revolutionary change, often with great bloodshed. Does it necessarily have to be this way?

Suppose that a democratic political system has been introduced on the island, and after several years of a government committed to central management, a pro-market party wins the elections. Just try to imagine what will become of the bureaucrats of Central Planning Committee and all the institutions they created to sustain the centrally managed system. And think of what will happen to all the entrepreneurial types who were previously suppressed and can now suddenly break out freely, to fulfill their destiny and talent?

The collapse of the communist economic system has taught us a great deal worth mentioning here. It exposed the incompetence of the previous ruling elites when faced with a competitive environment. They were too unimaginatively focused on manipulating political processes (solving political issues as explained before) and insufficiently oriented to the market to satisfy its needs and consumer demands. They were unable to act out of long-term responsibility. During the privatization process (the process of transferring ownership on business activities from government hands to private hands), it was often the managers who had been authorized to run economic concerns under the previous system that took over their ownership. In most cases they were very unsuccessful. Often they did not try to nourish and develop the companies they had suddenly acquired but just exploited them and stripped their assets, taking no responsibility for the liabilities. They were just unable to grasp the idea that the economic entity they were managing was their own.

And what about the transformation of a Market Economy into a Centrally Managed Economy? This definitely seems to have to be a revolutionary change. The government has to suppress private ownership. Private properties have to be confiscated or "nationalized". Price fixing has to be imposed on the suppliers. Laws suppressing private initiatives have to be passed and applied. New bureaucratic systems have to be created. All this demands so many legal changes and re-allocations of political and social position that I simply cannot see how it could ever happen without revolutionary upheaval, usually accompanied by bloodshed and suffering.

After much thought and an honest attempt to understand the phenomenon of widespread public support for dictatorships creating centrally managed economies, I can find very little positive to say about the centrally managed economic and governance system in terms of its practicality. I would probably agree that theoretically a centrally managed economy could implement long-term economic policy more easily, focusing on long-term aims. Yet historical experience with centrally managed economies has shown that in practice they have failed to achieve long-term goals. One example is environmental policy, which serves very long-term aims. The market economy has problems coping with it, but centrally managed economies have been even less successful. It should of course be admitted that the neglect of the environment by communist governments was more politically than economically motivated. The regimes did not cause the environmental neglect and damage out of the desire for personal gain such as increased profit or wealth, but to achieve the political goal of showing success in the competition with the economic achievements of the market economies.

In my view, the relative success of the centrally managed system in maintaining public support for so long term despite its obvious failure is to be explained by its apparent comprehensibility. It is easy to understand, and seems to have a simple internal mechanism, with a clear initiator and maintainer, as in most myths and religions. By contrast, the internal mechanism of the market economy is not at all obvious. After all, the "invisible hand" of the free market economy lacks the personality and purpose of gods and heroes, while the notion of a government that makes all the decisions and takes all the responsibilities is embedded in human mythic and epic consciousness. It is generally believed that every act has its activator, and it is always relatively hard to identify or perceive a self-igniting, self-managing system.

The market economy system rests on the idea that individual ownership, and individual enrichment making possible the accumulation of capital, is the basis for the economic efficiency of society as a whole. This idea is in turn premised on the assumption that the human individual acts out of a drive for ever more possessions, and that if successful he will enrich himself and by extension society as a whole, while if he fails his activity will be annihilated by the system itself. The void created by the annihilation of one entity will be filled by another more successful entity. As a consequence, resources that are being inefficiently used are released for more efficient exploitation. This system makes for a better utilization of limited resources across society, and increases its overall wealth. The necessary price to be paid to sustain this system is less evenly distributed wealth and income and continuous insecurity of employment.

Whereas the centrally managed communist system emphasizes the equal distribution of wealth and resources, the capitalistic market economy emphasizes personal liberty, including protection of personal possessions. Yet both political systems have tried to create a system of correct allocation of limited resources as efficiently as possible, and to redistribute economic wealth as evenly as possible. Both systems believe that equally distributed wealth is a positive value and should be stressed as a major political aim, even if the two systems disagree on the tools to be used to achieve this goal and the extent to which it can be achieved.

Contrary to general belief, the communist system actually failed to achieve the aim of more evenly distributed wealth. Statistics would probably show a more even distribution of income in the communist countries, but material well-being under the communist system was not easy to measure by such statistics. In terms of everyday life under the communist system, not only were the people generally poorer than in the capitalize market economy, but the differences between the ordinary people and those who were connected to the political elites were enormous. And it is a well-known sociological phenomenon that people's perception of being poor or rich is based on their income relative to others, rather than their absolute income.

Ordinary people were in practice not allowed to travel, but the communist elites were not subject to this rule. The rest of the population had to be satisfied with reading about the experiences of others, who were sent to crisscross the world to write books about exotic places. If the communist government functionaries thought these books would be a substitute for their subordinates' dreams of travel, they were mistaken. On the contrary, it just increased the travel fever of many young people, who used to risk their lives crossing barbed-wire because of their immense desire to experience the ultimate adventure, total freedom.

Since basic economic needs like housing were supplied by the government on the basis of administrative decisions and for prices under economic value, in practice the ordinary people were discriminated against compared to the communist elites, and this economic discrimination was not registered in the official statistics.

In centrally managed communist countries the ordinary people, who lacked access to the privileges of the elites, often had no way of satisfying quite basic needs. Their only way to get a bigger share of the collective cake was to ingratiate themselves with the officials authorized to control the resources.

Despite the communist belief in human willingness to act for a common purpose, most of the people authorized to manage the resources of the country abused the trust placed in them. No amount of control or supervision could prevent their exploitation of their position. Even if they did not officially own substantial private assets or receive a high salary, there were few limits to what they could obtain unofficially in perks, privileges and bribes. Most of them did not care if their acts caused misery to the others.

In my view human altruism increases with wealth, while poverty and misery are a major cause of cruelty and egotism. But then, you could rightly say that this kind of behavior is just human. Yet this is exactly the difference between the two systems. While the capitalist system accepts human beings with all their moral shortcomings, and accepts them as having only limited abilities to sacrifice for others, the communist system believed it was possible to remake human character to meet the highest standard of mutual altruism.

The human being is a socio-economic creature, with several contradictory attributes: Greed against Altruism, Competition against Cooperation, Individualism against Solidarity, Antagonism against Alliance, Heroism against Gutlessness, Resistance against Submissiveness.

We can then say that the most basic difference between the two economic ideologies is that while the so-called capitalist system tries to tame all these contradictory attributes and manipulate them by balancing between them, hoping for a positive outcome, the so-called communist system tries to fight and delegitimize the negative attributes of human character.

Yet all this does not exhaust the question of why a democratic, decentralized, market economy operates more efficiently and cost-effectively than a centrally managed economy.

The human urge for private possession seems to be universal, and seems to be connected to the basic desire of every individual for stability and security. Thus the first reason for the success of the market economy principle is that it recognizes the sacredness of private property. Belief in the property rights of those who have obtained their property as a reward for their entrepreneurial initiatives and risk-taking is one of the pillars of the achievements of the market economy. This ownership has to be unassailable.

On the other hand, this principle of private ownership and heritability of possessions naturally tends to lead to the accumulation of wealth in the hands of very few. The reason is the relative difficulty of joining the club of the wealthy, and the relative ease with which each its members can continue to generate more and more wealth. In the market economy it is the responsibility of a democratic government to help the poor to get out of the poverty trap created by this pattern of "to him that hath shall be given".

The process of the concentration of wealth in the economically well-established segment of society is usually disrupted at times of economic crisis, or major change in the economy such as a technological revolution, or change of political system. The computer and Internet revolution brought major shifts in the famous Forbes List of the wealthiest billionaires in the world. Sudden real estate price increase or collapse may have similar effects. But the most dramatic change in the Forbes list of billionaires is caused by sudden changes of political system. In times of peaceful stable economic development, the rise of new economic elites and the disappearance of the old elites is a gradual, incremental and even often marginal process. It is very different in times of revolutionary political change, when the existing ruling elites may be completely wiped out and replaced by new ones. The biggest upheaval in economic elites occurs when the whole economic system is changed, as happened in the last century with the dramatic changes in a large part of the world from market economy to centrally managed economy and later vice versa.

The second reason for the relative success of the market economy seems to be the way in which it nurtures and systematically rewards excellence, entrepreneurial spirit, initiatives, novelty and readiness to take risks. The market economy is a perfect system for adventurers, and less suitable for people of a more passive character. The market economy demands people educated enough to think for themselves and make their own decisions, and mainly to take responsibility for their actions, with all the pain that comes with having to admit failure as well.

The third reason seems to be connected with the insecurity generated by the market economy; continuous change and the fluidity of the demand for products means that suppliers must always be ready to respond if they want to survive as players in the market. The universal need to accumulate more and more wealth thus reflects the basic human desire for security rather than simply ambition. When the wealth he generates is more than an entrepreneur requires for his daily needs, it starts to accumulate and becomes capital invested in the next initiative, which it is hoped will lead to further growth in the wealth.

In contrast to the market economy, the centrally managed economies essentially seek to achieve the goal of an "Ideal Society". They therefore go with the kind of government that has a utopian vision. Once the ideal can be achieved there will be no reason to change it but merely to sustain it. The "Ideal Society" by definition has no need for any further change, and so the government aims its policy towards a steady state. To achieve this it has to create system of predefined, stable social, political and economic structures without dynamics. Such a system has difficulties adapting to change caused by unexpected factors, such as fashion, new technology, sudden demographic changes, and new ideas.

To try to sustain the centrally managed system, the government is forced to try to control every detail of the economy, society and individual life. It should not surprise anyone that all governments that have managed the economy centrally have limited the personal freedom of their citizens.

The result of governments with centrally managed economic systems is inevitably to freeze social and economic statuses (known as equality for all), and so private initiatives, entrepreneurial spirit and innovation are necessarily damaged and even destroyed. In other words, the government in centrally managed economies creates economic and social immobility, not only freezing economic innovation and dynamics but also imposing social ultra - conservatism and stagnation.

After mulling over the wise old man's long speech, the islanders created a new, democratic, market-oriented government. As might be expected, its first decision was to collect taxes.

To justify the tax collection in the eyes of the islanders, the government looked for important things to do with the money – things that non-government private entities, concerned above all with generating profits, would not want to do.

Inexperienced and confused about governing, the new island representatives turned again to the old wise man, and asked him, "What do the island and the islanders need a government for?"

The old man pondered for a while and then made a speech:

http://niv.scripturetext.com/1_samuel/8.htm

Samuel 8:4

When the elders of Israel gathered together and came to Samuel at Rama and said to him, appoint a king to lead us, such as all the other nations have. "Give us a king to lead us," this displeased Samuel; so he prayed to the Lord. And the Lord told him: "Listen to all that the people are saying to you; it is not you they have rejected, but they have rejected me as their king. As they have done from the day I brought them up out of Egypt until this day, forsaking me and serving other gods, so they are doing to you. Now listen to them; but warn them solemnly and let them know what the king who will reign over them will do."

Samuel said to the people, "This is what the king who will reign over you will do: He will take your sons and make them serve with his chariots and horses, and they will run in front of his chariots. Some he will assign to be commanders of thousands and commanders of fifties, and others to plow his ground and reap his harvest, and still others to make weapons of war and equipment for his chariots. He will take your daughters to be perfumers and cooks and bakers. He will take the best of your fields and vineyards and olive groves and give them to his attendants. He will take a tenth of your grain and of your vintage and give it to his officials and attendants. Your menservants and maidservants and the best of your cattle and donkeys he will take for his own use. He will take a tenth of your flocks, and you yourselves will become his slaves. When that day comes, you will cry out for relief from the king you have chosen, and the Lord will not answer you in that day."

But the people refused to listen to Samuel and said. "We want to be like any other nations, with a king to lead us and to go out before us and fight our battles."

The islanders listened attentively, but their expressions betrayed a certain puzzled incredulity, so the old man continued: "You probably did not get what I was saying so let me try another parable":

http://niv.scripturetext.com/judges/9.htm

Judges 9:7

Jotham the priest climbed up on the top of mount and shouted, "Listen to me, citizens";

One day the trees went out to anoint a king for themselves. They said to the olive tree, „Be our king." "But the olive tree answered, „Should I give up my oil, by which both gods and men are honored, to hold sway over the trees?"

"Next, the trees said to the fig tree, „Come and be our king." "But the fig tree replied, „Should I give up my fruit, so good and sweet, to hold sway over the trees?"

"Then the trees said to the vine, „Come and be our king." "But the vine answered, „Should I give up my wine, which cheers both gods and men, to hold sway over the trees?"

"Finally all the trees said to the thorn bush, „Come and be our king." "The thorn bush said to the trees, „If you really want to anoint me king

over you, come and take refuge in my shade; but if not, then let fire come out of the thorn bush and consume all of you!"

Noticing the rather blank stare of the islanders, the old man pondered for a while, sighed and said:

"If there must be a government, let it be the least vile government possible; let it be a liberal service supplier, democratically elected government.

If a democratically elected government wants to be a good government, it has to regard itself as a service supplier and not as a governor or ruler. A service-supplier government has three major tasks to fulfill;

The first task of a government is to secure the legal system, with rules and laws to define rights and obligations. The laws will have to apply equally to every private person or private entity on the island, and even to the government itself and its members. These obligations and rules will be defined by House of Representatives, a legislative body that will represent the island's citizens and will be elected by the islanders. This representation will as far as possible reflect the whole spectrum of Islander society.

The law created by these representatives will embody the moral codes derived from the islanders' traditions, ethics, conventions, beliefs, knowledge and so on. If there are disagreements between elected members of the legislative body, and they have different ideas representing different interests or different sections of island society (net weavers against fishermen), the dispute will be decided by a majority of the legislative body, but with efforts to take minority opinions into account rather than simply roll over them. One of the basic principles upholding the legal system will be equality before the law and equality of economic opportunity for all the islanders, without regard to social and economic origin and status. The government will then have to create an instrument to ensure that the law functions properly, punishing people who violate the law, and protecting those who honor the law. The government in a market economy acts under legal directives created by the legislative institution, the House of Representatives, which is elected in order to create a legal framework for a fair economic environment, which means law applying to and enforced equally on every economic entity.

The second task of the government is to protect the islanders from external and internal threats to their security. This means the government must create a police force, with a unique monopoly on the use of force to protect islanders according to the laws passed. The government will also have to create a military force capable of defending the islanders from potential external intruders. It will have to make sure that the military and the police force act in line with the policy of the government and House of Representatives and do not abuse their legal monopoly of coercive force to trample on the rights of the islanders. To ensure the neutrality of the security forces in potential conflicts between the islanders and the island government, or between different sections of islander society, the military and police will operate under very strict supervision established by the laws and enforced by an independent judiciary, which will implement the laws against any wrongdoings by individuals in the military and police services. Compared to civil society, the potential destructive power of the police and army is almost unlimited. To prevent misuse of this imbalance of power in the country, their actions must be continuously supervised and subject to tight controls.

The third task of the government is to create a social system of mutual aid, whereby the strong and economically capable will support the less capable. The market economy by its nature provides better opportunities to economically capable and strong individuals and entities, and without government intervention they get their hands on most of the economic resources. The government's task is to restrain this tendency and to foster solidarity among the islanders by supporting the weak and poor as against the strong sections of society. The government does so by intervening in different fields of activity, such as:

1. Ensuring that everyone receives a basic education. It must also support higher education and institutions of knowledge responsible for preserving, accumulating and developing knowledge and distributing it to present and coming generations of islanders. It may also support mutual exchange of knowledge with the mainlanders, on the understanding that this exchange will have a positive effect in the island but also on the mainland. If the Islanders come up with some unique advance in the field of the knowledge, it will increase the prestige of the islanders among the mainlanders and enhance the islanders' self-confidence.

2. Securing basic health services for all. Even if this may seem self-evident, it raises many problems. Giving the right to medical treatment inevitably rises the question, how much medical treatment can be secured to everyone. Some medical treatment may be too expensive to be offered free to everyone, and so only those few individuals who can afford to pay for it will be able to receive it. Whether to provide all scientifically available medical treatment to everybody or restrict free healthcare is a question of economics and not just morality. At the end of the day, there will be medical treatments that will have to be denied to some of the islanders, because otherwise these few very expensive medical treatments will swallow up most of the resources allocated for healthcare. If no limits are created, medical services may become so costly that the islanders are no longer ready to pay for them via taxation or insurance and this may eventually cause regression in general medical treatment for most of the islanders.

3. Securing a minimum income for islanders who are economically unable to take care of themselves: the disabled, the sick, the old who contributed their share to society in the past and now need support in their turn, and newborn children and their families. The government must also provide a minimum income for islanders who are temporarily unemployed and basic accommodation for those who cannot afford it for themselves and would otherwise be homeless. Since payment for all

these services will come out of taxes, and in principle more tax is collected from the richer citizens while the poorer make more use (or at least equal use) of government services, all these services help to redistribute the wealth of the island more evenly. Yet when deciding on the right dosage of mutual aid policy the government has to remember that transferring wealth from the rich to the poor means transferring resources from the rich to the poor. To most islanders that may sound all to the good, but such a transfer of resources also means less in the way of savings. When resources remain in the hands of the wealthy, it is very likely that more will be saved and less will be immediately consumed. After all not even the wealthiest man can sit in more than one chair or sleep in more than one bed, so most of his income will not be spent and will remain as capital for investment to generate increased wealth in the future. The other disadvantage of redistribution of wealth by administrative means is that it has a negative impact on the entrepreneurs' tendency to initiate new ventures and take risks. More resources saved and increased encouragement for entrepreneurial spirit means that in the future there will be more resources available for economic entities that will eventually enlarge the economic platform of the island, and increase the future tax base.

Still, on the personal level, government members and officials are socially more closely associated with the strong and economically well-off elites of the island than with the poorer masses. How can we make sure that the government will do its best to implement a policy of mutual aid and welfare rather than furthering the interests of friends, relations and cronies? The answer is to have a government that is democratically elected and subject to re-election after a set time. At the end of its fixed term of office, the government has to give the islanders the right to express their satisfaction or dissatisfaction with its record freely. The islanders' representatives and the government itself have to periodically submit themselves to the judgment of the islanders, who have the chance to endorse or reject the existing government. The islanders make their decision by majority vote on who will sit in the next House of Representatives and the next government. Naturally, the majority of the islanders are the middle and the low income level segment of the society and not the elites. If the government does not attend to the needs of the majority and make a sincere effort to balance income and wealth between the different islanders, it will probably have a hard time getting re-elected.

4. One activity that tends to be the responsibility of governments is to invest in fields important for general prosperity but unattractive to the private sector because the rate of return is too long-term and the financial risk too great, or because the investment required is beyond private capacity. These sorts of projects are usually very large-scale or nationwide, such as intercity highways and railways, hydroelectric plants, the electricity grid, entirely new settlements and so on.

Here are some more specific examples of typical government investment areas:

1. Basic scientific research that has no direct economic impact but can lead to major scientific breakthroughs and eventually change the paradigm of the lives of the islanders and the mainlanders too. Sometimes the utility of such scientific findings is not immediately clear and cannot be economically exploited in the short-term, yet its indirect impact on human life can be enormous. The very best example is the equation $E=MC^2$. It did not have any practical impact when first published, but later changed the whole paradigm of future human life.

2. Building national roads, ports, and other infrastructure where the return on investment takes a very long time, sometimes more than a generation, and the economic impact and added value is not only direct (in the form of tolls on eventual users), but also indirect (increase in connectivity among the islanders and between the islanders and the mainlanders, with a positive effect on the islanders' perception and understanding of realities beyond the island itself).

3. Building hydroelectric plants and other facilities that are just too large

and expensive in terms of capital to be funded by a private entity. Also, plants of this kind usually have an indirect environmental impact, and a profit-orientated private entity might well be tempted to neglect consideration of these long-term potential impacts, whereas government is supposed to have responsibilities beyond short-term profit, at least in principle.

When government is not busy with war or building big national projects, it still needs to provide services for political as well as economic purposes. The best example is education, which from the government's point of view is not just a source of economic benefits for the island and its people, but a way to raise a new generation of supporters of the country and its political system. The government leaders hope that if suitably educated, the young will become soldiers of the island, increase its security and follow in the footsteps of their elders. (Fortunately, in reality this rarely happens, because in the modern world each generation has an entirely different way of thinking and doing things.)

All the services the Government is expected or keen to supply could in principle be supplied by private entities, but private entities act out of a desire to maximize profit, and in as short a time as possible, whereas the government should act out of long-term vision. When it provides obligatory education for all children, it acts out of concern to produce a future generation educated enough to take over the running of the island. When it provides healthcare for all, even if not every kind of medical treatment is available for all, or when it guarantees a minimum income to all, it gives the islanders a feeling of security, and this increases their sense of belonging and identification with the island and its institutions.

If the government wants to enlarge the island's economic platform, it has to invest today with a view to achieving more production capacity in the future. But to invest also means not consuming all the resources now, but putting some of them aside, i.e. saving. In other words to accumulate unused resources, to accumulate CAPITAL that will be used to create new enterprises or expand existing enterprises. This enlargement of the economic platform, or economic growth, will expand the economy, bringing future benefits to all the islanders and to the government as well by securing increased income from future taxes.

This accumulation of Capital also exists in a centrally managed economy, with the difference that there the decisions about how and where to invest are concentrated solely in the hands of the government, while in the market economy it remains in the hands of various different private entities, who use it for new ventures or for further development of their businesses. Supporters of the market economy believe that the concentration of the accumulated capital in the hands of the relatively numerous successful entrepreneurs will make its allocation more efficient than if it were placed solely in the hands of government.

The centrally managed economic system involves the concentration of the authority in the hands of very few, and these few have a natural tendency to focus their attention on rather large projects, neglecting the small. The result in communist countries was the concentration of economic, mainly production capacities, in mega-sized facilities that served most of the market with their products.

I remember reading Boris Yeltsin's rather humorous account of how as Major of Sverdlovsk (Yekaterinburg), he persuaded Brezhnev, then the actual head of the Soviet dictatorship, to invest in a project to construct a city metro. He describes how he patiently waited for just the right time to approach Brezhnev, when the leader was drunk but not too drunk to sign the papers needed to start the metro project. Yeltsin was very successful, and Sverdlovsk became the second city right after Moscow to get a metro. But the story tells us a great deal more about the decision-making process than that. And was it right that Sverdlovsk should have got a metro before Leningrad (Sankt Petersburg), a much bigger city?

The obvious primary economic function of the government is to regulate the economy so as to prevent sudden disturbances in the equilibrium state between the volume of money and the product value in circulation. The government's problem, unfortunately, is that it is hard to predict how the economy will respond to such corrective efforts, because of the slow and uncertain reaction of Product as compared to the speedy reaction of Money to economic policy changes. Even if the economy responds to the policy by moving in the right direction, it will take too long for the results to be seen and felt by the public.

The delay between the measures taken by the government and central bank to change the volume of money in circulation and hence the volume of product value in circulation, and any visible improvement in the economy, may be one to two years or even more. Consequently, the results of measures taken by the government are usually visible only after the next general election. This is very inconvenient for the decision-making politicians, who are judged by the public not on the basis of the correctness of the policies that they actually adopted, but instead by immediate and recent economic developments, which are largely results of measures taken by the previous government.

To make things even worse, it is rarely obvious which measure taken by which government caused a positive or negative economic correction when it eventually occurs. The misfortunes of US President George Bush Senior are a good illustration of the problem. As president in 1990, he faced increasing national debt and a deficit that seemed to be out of control. He worked out a plan of tax increases and spending cuts that could have ended the federal deficit within a few years, but in the short term the US economy went into a deep slowdown and George Bush Senior was not re-elected to a second term. If he had been re-elected and continued his economic policy, maybe the huge US deficit, which is one of the main reasons for the instability in the world economy since 2008, would not exist. But he lost the elections. Later his "mistake" was "corrected" by his son George W. Bush, whose policy as president of the USA caused a skyrocketing government budget deficit, but on the other hand ensured that young Dubya was easily re-elected for a second term.

This time delay between the implemented government policy and the results, caused partly by the mismatch between the reactivity of Money and Product, makes government austerity measures very unpopular. After all, austerity measures mean government budget cuts to services supplied to the people and/or tax increases. No electorate, even if supportive of a policy opposing government deficits and the notion of a balanced government budget and small government, really likes the pain caused by government expenses cuts that mean less education, less healthcare, less police, but also less government activity, and so fewer chances for government subcontractors and fewer and less well-paid jobs for government employees.

It is no surprise that elected governments usually like to leave the economic response to sudden changes in macroeconomic circumstances to the Central Bankers, who operate with "speedy" Money and not with "lazy" Product. Governments hope that the inevitable criticism will be diverted from themselves to the governor of the central bank and to the commercial banks. After all, the bankers are appointed and don't have to answer to any electorates.

While in a Centralized Economic System the government intentionally creates economic entities with the position of sole supplier, in the Market Economy a basic principle of legislation is to prevent the existence of sole suppliers (or monopolies). One of the challenges faced by government is how to avoid unjust bias in the legal system, giving an advantage to one economic entity over another, and to prevent the unfair practices of dominant economic players who try to annihilate competition by lobbying for legislation that gives them an advantage over their competitors. The challenge is even greater when the dominant economic player in a certain field is the government itself, often effectively in the position of a monopoly.

Unlike private enterprise, government activity is financed by tax collection and not by direct collection of payment from the final consumer. The tax is collected from private enterprise, and so if the government insists on rights of exclusive activity in an area, it has to justify them. This justification is particularly obvious, but can also be particularly problematic, in fields where the government has a special interest, like the military and police force.

Democratic states are most politically successful when they manage to foster a broad band of middle-class population, which is well educated and, even if it is not part of the ruling elite, feels it has a good chance of one day becoming so. In this situation the middle class regards itself as related to the ruling class, and its members believe that if they try hard enough they can rise to the very top. If this feeling of having a chance to enter the island's ruling elites, and being part of the political decision-making process, is common among a large enough number of islanders, it will become a main pillar of the support of all the islanders for the political system, even when they do not necessarily support the policy of the current leadership. If sufficiently widespread, the perception of participation in the political process neutralizes radical political opposition. Most of the revolutions of modern times have happened when a government has failed to apply the law equally to everybody and has not given the majority of the population a feeling of potential participation in government and policy-making.

The Market Economy, being based on competition and excellence, encourages the rise of economic elites generating privately owned assets and wealth, and accumulating privately owned capital that will be used in the future for investments and development. By contrast the goal of a government running a centrally managed economy is to create evenly distributed rewards for everyone, and so it actively prevents the accumulation of economic wealth in the hands of private entities.

Every democratic government wants to be popular with the majority of the people, and since social services are provided to a wide range of people, while social taxation is mostly paid for by relatively narrow group of economic elites, the government has a tendency to provide many more and more generous services than it can pay for out of the taxes it collects. Increased services demand an increased level of taxation, and excessive taxation can cause disruption to the economic activity of the economic entities paying those taxes. They may lose their motivation for entrepreneurship, innovation, investment and further development, and if this happens the economic base for tax collection will shrink. Government solves the problem by providing "More" services to the population than the taxes it collects. This "More" is called the "Government Deficit".

In principle, nothing is wrong with government deficit when it is financed by bank loans that can be repaid, just so long as government activity also includes investments that will increase the economic potential in the future, and with it an increased economic base for additional future government income from taxes. Just as a private enterprise, which invests borrowed money in a new venture can repay the money with the additional income the loan will help it to generate, the future rise in government income can in principle cover the repayment of these loans. In this context it would be advisable for government to use loans taken from the commercial banks for investments creating potential economic growth, and not for expanding the services it provides to the population, which may have only very small long-term impact on economic growth, if any.

The problem is that by taking loans from commercial banks, the government competes for financial resources with private companies, and this drives up interest rates for private companies. Competition with government for financial resources may well cause a squeeze on the private sector's capacity to get loans. This naturally reduces the private entities' business activities and the associated potential economic growth. In the long run, the result of this form of financing the government deficit will be the same as taxation. In principle, if the government increases its activity without creating an enlarged platform for additional economic activity in the private sector and hence economic growth, this will always be at someone else's expense.

The squeeze on the private sector has a negative impact on the government's future capacity to collect taxes. To avoid this, governments usually try to trick the system and instead of taking loans from the commercial banks or raising taxes they issue government debt securities. This form of financing does not compete directly with private entities for the financial resources of the commercial banks, but it competes with other forms of finance, like corporate debt securities, and so in the long run it will produce the same effect of relative squeeze on the private sector.

In the short run, different systems of financing a government deficit create different results. For example, income tax is an obvious way to finance government activities, but income tax is a tax imposed on every individual or private economic entity and its rate increases in parallel with increase in income. This means that in the short term the effect of raising income tax will be to de-motivate individuals and entities from increased efforts to generate additional income. The sum of the incomes of all individuals and entities is equivalent to the national income and to the national product. So at the end of the day, the reduced tendency of many individuals to create additional income reduces the national product, or what we call in this book the aggregate volume of product value in circulation.

Increased income tax also reduces the disposable income of the individual and hence consumer spending. Yet the income tax collected is injected back into the economy by government activity, and so has less influence on consumption than taxes on products, which cause immediate price increase for those products. If the tax raised is the corporate tax, the measure reduces the willingness of corporations to invest. If the deficit is financed by some form of money printing, the result will be what we call in this book the "money comes first" situation, and as we have discovered, if this is excessive it will inevitably cause a general increase in the prices of the products, or in other words inflation.

Inflation itself is kind of taxation imposed by the government on the islanders. Direct taxation is based on income, property ownership or product consumption, and is therefore levied mostly from the more affluent. If the tool chosen by the government to cover its deficit is Inflation, this will be imposed on the population indirectly, without the government's control and regulation and without public discussion and approval. It therefore affects the islanders arbitrarily; the worst hit are not necessarily those who are the most able to pay. Most probably, the "Inflation tax" will fall more heavily on the poorer islanders whose assets are mainly in the form of cash money or current deposits in the banks, which loses its value with Inflation, than on the rich islanders, who are more protected because they own different forms of assets with a value that usually appreciates with the Inflation.

So it is clear that whatever the government increases its expenditure and this increase is not stimulating economic growth, ultimately this will be at the expense of the private sector. This problem is another aspect of the essential economic phenomenon we mentioned at the beginning of the book, "The effect of the short blanket". In other words, if the government increases its activity when the island production capacity is fully employed, this will have a negative effect on private sector activity, and squeeze its relative size, regardless of how the increased government expenses are funded.

The worst scenario caused by government activity is when government takes out loans that are wasted on useless or counter-productive investments, known as "white elephant projects". There are many examples of governments investing billions of dollars in projects that are never completed, or even worse are completed but never become operational because the income or the benefit they generate is less than the maintenance costs. These investments will probably never enlarge the economic platform of a country and its tax base.

Interesting historical examples of white elephant projects, but with a very surprising eventual outcome, were the Gothic churches built all over Europe in the High Middle Ages. Some estimate that at the time when their building peaked, they used up a quarter of all economic resources while at the time adding very little to an economy faced primarily with the problem of producing enough food, to prevent mass starvation, and accumulating enough gold to pay soldiers in their continual wars. Yet this example also highlights the oddities created by the changing world in the long run. These churches, located in the heart of towns and cities, provided a substantial impulse to urban development, which brought advances in European civilization and had a major impact on the economic metamorphosis of the continent.

As has been said, in a Market Economy the government is one of the players in the game of providing products, mainly in form of services to the population. When fulfilling this task, it is expected to avoid competition with private entities. You may rightly ask why the government should avoid competition with private entities?

The first reason is that it would be a very unfair practice for the government to compete with those who are obliged to pay the taxes that finance its activity.

The second reason is that whereas private suppliers have to operate in the context of continuous comparison of their performance with that of other suppliers, and under constant threat of liquidation if they make wrong decisions, government can carry on regardless of the mistaken decisions it made and the consequent negative results of its activity. After all, the government as a supplier of product is not usually paid directly, and does not have to confront the consumer; even in cases where it generates some direct income from a product, it does not have to cover all the costs involved in its production. The government's costs are covered by the taxes it collects in line with the legislation it initiates. The purpose of these taxes is rarely directly specified and connected to any specific service.

The third reason is that in most cases consumption of the government product is obligatory; the consumer does not have the right of free choice as to whether or not to use it. Just think about it, when have you ever made a decision to consume military or police services? If you cannot remember doing that, don't worry as you probably never took such a decision – the use of those services is just imposed on you by the government. By the way, in principle the army and police exist to defend the whole population from threats and even atrocities by internal or external enemies. Yet it is often used to defend the government itself from the anger of the population, provoked by the wrongdoings of government itself. The discontented masses may sometimes become unmanageable, creating political chaos that can end in an uprising against the ruling elites, who may even be destroyed. Since every government represents a certain ruling economic elite, its natural tendency is to try to prevent widespread public anger. Yet if a government fails to forestall an uprising of the masses, it may be swept away together with the political and economic elites with which it is identified.

After such a revolution, when public anxiety and public anger calms down or the public is exhausted by events and is looking for some form of stability and security, a new leader or leadership usually appears and imposes a new ruling elite instead of the old one. Since the new ruling elite needs to strengthen and legitimize its political position, it tends to be more repressive then the previous one and a great deal more murderous.

Even if they never admit it, some governments think that their main task is to prevent any turbulence or uprising among the masses and to protect the ruling elites from them. This kind of connection between a dominant economic entity and the political leadership creates a system of plutocracy, where the ruling elite of oligarchs is disconnected from the rest of the society. If it fails to change its attitude from time to time, such an oligarchy may in the end be discarded and annihilated by the masses, whose interests the oligarchs have neglected in their policy. This is why every government is very sensitive to any public criticism, tries to prevent it and sometimes even fights against it. The government also acts in different ways to do everything needed to keep the mass public satisfied (or at least to make a show of doing so, and to create an attractive and reassuring public image of concern and responsibility).

The fourth point is that usually the government's activity is not directly connected to your personal needs, but to the needs of the whole island population or a certain segment of the population, and you as an individual are not necessarily interested in this specific service. A very good example is external security, which requires the maintenance of armed forces, while you may happen to be a pacifist. Even if you don't approve of this particular service provided by the government, and even feel antagonism towards its supporters, you still have to pay taxes that go to support this activity. Another example is unemployment benefit, which often angers the employed, who pay their taxes regularly and can feel robbed of part of their hard -earned income for the sake of people they may see as feckless and idle.

The last but not the least reason to prevent the government competing freely with a private entity is the relative inefficiency of the government as a product supplier compared to the private entity. If government and a private entity both supply the same product, the private entity will always be more efficient, and will provide better and cheaper products.

Why is it that the government as service provider is usually less efficient than a private entity? After all, government employees are not necessarily less talented than those employed in private entities. Very often when a government employee switches to a job in a privately owned company, he finds he starts to act more effectively and efficiently.

The problem seems to be more structural than individual. Probably the main reason is that government has difficulty clearly identifying its goals. It is generally understood that organizations which clearly define their goals, and successfully encourage their managers and employees to serve these goals, will be more successful than organizations that do not. Unlike private entities, whose main goal is profitability, the government with its wide responsibilities has difficulty defining its priorities in the same exact way. This is also why when a government-owned entity is privatized, the private owner will cut costs and activities that are less or not profitable. When a production facility run by the government has to reduce its production capacity because there is no need for its products, the government will do all it can to avoid firing the workers (for nobody knows how many electors are behind each worker). By contrast, private employers are motivated mainly by profit, and so if they fail to cut production capacities and use of resources when demand for their product declines, their profits will drop and their very existence could be endangered. The continuous need for an economically active privately owned entity to react to the changing market environment correctly and promptly, because otherwise its existence will be threatened, is one of the basic blocks of the market economy.

The annihilation or bankruptcy of an economic entity is not a fault or malfunction of the market economic system, but one of its basic pillars. I have to emphasize again and again that if an economic entity produces products that the market does not want, or if it cannot produce them for a price similar to its competitors, this entity has to cease to exist, or in other words go bankrupt. It is a very cruel rule, but the destruction of the incompetent and release of space and resources for the existing or newly born competent is the instrument ensuring the health and vitality of the economy. An economic entity producing products that are old - fashioned, inefficient and so not in demand is bound to die. It is just the same as in nature: everything has to die to give space to the new-born, the strong dispose of the weak, and inefficient entities are doomed. Any economic policy that seeks to prevent this circle of economic life is predestined to self-destruction.

Another reason why government activity is inefficient is its tendency to operate under protective legislation. Like any other entrepreneur the government dislikes competition, yet unlike a private entrepreneur the government can create laws to limit competition. This has been the case with too many government activities in the past.

One good example is telephone communications before the arrival of the mobile phone. Just a few decades ago some countries had laws stipulating that not only the phone grid, but also the phone apparatus and the wire connecting the phone apparatus to the grid in private homes, was the property of the national telephone company. If you thought the traditional black dial phone predominated until recent times because of technological limitations, you were mistaken. It was in fact illegal to change it. The repeal of this law caused a highly visible change. Suddenly people could have telephones in colors other than the traditional black one, and with push buttons instead of the traditional dial. But the real revolution came when governments privatized national telephone companies and turned them into stock companies driven by profit. Suddenly all those people who had been having to wait 5-10 years for a phone line got one immediately, and were even directly offered a second line. Then of course came mobile phones, and nobody needed fixed lines anymore anyway. For a very similar reason, if you move from one country to another one, even within the European Union, you cannot just use your electrical equipment by plugging it into the nearest socket. You will often need an adaptor, which is hard to find. Every country has its government-owned and managed electric company, which operates under laws of protection including the right to decide what sort of plug will be legal in the country. If someone tells you that the electric plugs in his country are the safest anywhere, don't believe him, because all the plugs are the same.

Another reason for relative government inefficiency is the lack of measurable results by which government activity can be judged and its employees rewarded or punished. Whereas a private economic entity is judged and rewarded or punished according to its profit or loss, or its balance of assets and liabilities, government activity cannot be judged in such a way. Even if it tries to operate according to market economy rules, government organizational structure is bureaucratic and its activities are run within a rigid system of regulations. It is a centrally managed system, with all its follies. If no continuous new reforms are imposed on it, the system fossilizes through over-bureaucratization and over-regulation, until its real aim is lost and self-perpetuation of the system becomes its only objective. One very famous example of this process of fossilization of government activity is the British Colonial Office during and after the process of decolonization of the British Empire. Even when the British Empire was gone, the British Colonial Office continued to increase the number of its employees.

This difficulty of relating rewards and penalties to achievements and failures at any organizational level of government activity is a major obstacle to efficiency. To prevent criticism for misuse of taxpayers' money, governments draw up very strict codes setting out what its offices and staff can and cannot do. The government imposes a strict wage scale, usually based not on employee performance but on seniority, or official education level. If no continuous new reforms are imposed on the government, over-bureaucratization and over-regulation are inevitable.

Unlike a private entrepreneur, who when fulfilling an order to a consumer is in direct contact with him, government supplies services to consumers who are anonymous tax-payers. But who is the tax-payer? Sometimes we read in the news about a tax evader caught by the tax authorities, but have you ever read about someone because he was an ordinary tax-payer? This anonymity of the tax-payers means that the government as a service supplier tends to be indifferent or sluggish when it supplies the product.

In theory, the politicians responsible for government activities will be rewarded by re -election if they fulfill the expectations of the voters. But can voters recognize which government's decision caused which result?

As we observed earlier, the time schedule of economic cycles of prosperity and crisis and prosperity again are desynchronized from the decisions that actually cause these cycles. If an economic boom with full employment arrives, the public will associate it with the present government, even though it is well known that major economic policy changes take years to produce results. This long lag between the decision of the government and the consequences of its decision is only one problem when it comes to judging the government's performance. A bigger problem is the great range of subjects on which the government has to take decisions, so that even if one decision has negative results, another may seem to be bringing benefits.

The very awareness of time delay and the difficulty of identifying which decisions have had economically calamitous consequences can prompt the disastrous decisions that many governments make when they are trying to court popularity. Governments tend to make popular decisions which on the surface look very positive in the eyes of the public, and have an immediate short-term positive effect, but are very damaging on the long term.

The most problematic decisions of this kind are the food and energy subsidies mostly operated in underdeveloped poor countries. They have had several bad results. The artificially low prices of food and energy cause wastage and overconsumption of these items, but also a reluctance on the part of farmers or energy suppliers to increase their output of the subsidized products. The worst happens when there is further increase in the world commodity prices connected to the subsidized products. Since the population is used to governmental responsibility for fixing food and energy prices, if the government reacts to the world commodity price increase by raising the fixed price, it is blamed by the population. To avoid the unpopularity and its political consequences, the government tends to increase the subsidy level, so that the government deficit grows and eventually a "money comes first" situation develops. This may be followed by general price increase of all the products except those that the government subsidizes. But now to keep the subsidized product prices stable, the government has to increase the volume of subsidies even further. And the spiral described in chapter 3 starts to rotate.

But if you think that subsidy policies only exist in poor underdeveloped countries, you are mistaken. Recently the rich countries, mainly the European Union states, decided to subsidize green and sustainable energy sources without carefully calculating the potential results. The aim of the policy was to help to develop technologies that are ecologically positive and based on sustainable sources. Most of the subsidies went on installing photo-panel technologies which directly convert sunlight to electricity. Unfortunately the relatively high cost of these technologies meant that the government subsidies were huge, and their impact on the environment has been turning out to be more negative than positive. In certain very surprising cases these plants were discovered to be generating "solar energy" at night. Guess how.....By projecting artificial light on the solar panels.

In terms of cost effectiveness, the subsidies were a failure. Governments would definitely achieve much better results by pouring only a fraction of these subsidies directly into research. The huge price difference between the new technology and the old technology also meant that more energy had to be invested in the new technological solution. If the comprehensive environmental impact of these new technologies were calculated, the result would most probably be negative.

If to summarize into few major issues the question what is the main difference between the economic entities run by government and those privately owned, the answer would probably be;

While the government activity is financed by taxes collected from large parts of the population, and not necessarily all of them are consumers of the government's products, the privately owned economic entity is totally dependent on its consumers demand. Even if the government fails to attract sufficient demand for its activity, it still can continue its existence, while if the private entity fails to attract sufficient demand, eventually it will have to perish.

The second important difference between the two is that while the privately owned economic activity can attract private financial resources only by generating high yield on investment with apparently low risk, the finances raised as taxes doesn't have to generate yield at all.

In spite of all the reasons against, governments do have a tendency to compete with private entities and provide the same services to the islanders as the private sector. On the other hand, in past decades there has been a major reaction against governments as service providers, and politicians have adopted a policy of transferring government provider organizations into private hands. This process is called privatization. Amazingly, when privatization is carried out, and this has happened in many sectors including most famously telecommunications, transport, postal services, medical institutions and even schools, the result has been increased efficiency in the sector or organization concerned, just by becoming private.

But the process of privatization does not always result in more efficiency and better service for the benefit of the general public. The act of privatization has to be accompanied by parallel decisions that will correct the circumstances under which the government operated. The most important is to cancel special rights that protected the government operation from competition. If for example the subject of privatization is some natural monopoly like the electric company or water, drainage, sewerage systems, it is important to ensure that the prices charged by the new private companies will either be regulated by the government, or that the privatization will be carried out in such a way that the new providers of these services will have to compete with each other for clients.

"Illekoshtujet", those were the very first words I heard in Poland, back in the sixties when as a teenage boy I crossed the border from Slovakia to Poland with some friends and immediately encountered Polish hawkers who tried to buy the clothes right off our backs. In Slovakia, which had a much more rigid communist system than Poland and allowed no private enterprise, we had never encountered the phenomenon of someone asking "what is the price?" Prices were given and never argued about.

The basic tool of the market economy for the co-ordination of use of resources is the floating price of products. Even if you have the impression that prices are steady, in a market economy they are constantly changing in response to the changing economic realities, or what economists call change in demand and supply. The prices are the automatic regulator that puts products on the shelves of the stores just in time and always in the right quantity and quality demanded by the consumer.

Have you ever asked yourself how come, whenever you want to purchase one of the hundreds of thousands of products available to purchase, you can almost always find it somewhere, unless you are looking for some very, very peculiar product?

If you are fond of conspiracy theories, which are essentially based on the belief that everything in this world is managed by some kind of hidden mysterious manager giant, or worse, some hidden evil, you will be disappointed by what I have to say next. But here it is: **The availability of all the products you purchase, like the milk you purchase every day, or the wedding anniversary gift you purchase once a year, or the house you purchase probably only once in your life time, all for a relatively steady price, is a kind of miracle that happens every day, and without any centrally located director regulating it or making any decisions about it.**

It is amazing that it is enough just to let the product price change freely and all the shelves of the shops will be full of more goods than a normal human can take in. And it is even more amazing that whenever a centrally managed body, a government or an institution empowered by the government, or in other words a "Mysterious Manager Giant", tries to determine the product price to create available Products for all consumers for a reduced price, it always fails, and always ends up the same way. With endless lines of potential consumers, queuing patiently or impatiently to enter a shop, hoping to purchase products that seem not to have been produced in sufficient quantities, while on the corner close to the shop some black-market dealers always have enough of the same Product for double or triple the price.

The communist empire never could solve the problem of these queues of impatient consumers, and in the end it was these queues for basic life necessities that caused the collapse of the whole Empire, in most areas without a single shot fired. All the enormous military power that the communist state had accumulated could not prevent this collapse.

It is not that they did not try to solve the problem of the long lines in front of the shops. They did everything they could. They even sent policemen to register the citizens standing in the lines in front of the shops, and threaten them with punishment. But nothing helped to solve the problem of fulfilling the needs of the citizens, because the only measure that would have worked was the one they did not try: to end the fixing of product prices. They realized that doing so would be an admission that their whole centrally managed economy was a mistake and all the suffering it had caused for the people of their countries had been for nothing but a very bad farce.

After the communist governments had for decades pretended they had found the miracle cure for all economic ills: - the elixir of price stability, full employment, and secure income stability - it is not so very surprising that they were unable to abandon the very basics of their economic system, the fixed product prices, and adopt the floating price system. The communist leaders forced the whole population to believe in this folly, mostly by criminal acts against those courageous enough to ask questions about the discrepancies of the system. The obstinacy of the communist leaders had grown over time as the sufferings of the population increased. People often close their eyes to obvious realities rather than admit their mistakes, but the communist regimes took this common human fault to extreme lengths.

In fact a psychologically similar phenomenon can sometimes be observed in market economies, when business executives in the market economy refuse to admit having made bad investments, keep trying to cover up for too long and end up causing huge losses to the companies they manage. Even more surprising is the implementation of product price control policy by governments claiming to be bastions of the market economy, like the US government. One of the most bizarre examples is the price control imposed on petrol prices in 1973 after the October war in the Middle East and subsequent massive increase in the price of oil by the oil producers. It very soon caused long queues at petrol stations. In the end, the real prices paid for petrol (including the cost of the time spent waiting in line) were often higher than they would have been if the price had not been controlled.

In most cases the justification for price control is the desire to achieve a more equal distribution of income at times of crisis. The crisis may be caused by events like a harvest failure after catastrophically unfavorable weather conditions, war, or other events that disrupt the supply chain of a very basic product. Realizing the sudden imperative to satisfy everybody's basic needs, the government reacts to these events by price control as a temporary measure until the crisis passes. If used as a temporary tool, price control can be understandable and even effective.

But when the crisis is finally over, the government may have difficulty entirely lifting price controls because the resulting price increase will inevitably be very unpopular, and so it may decide to keep price control as a government tool to redistribute the resources more equally. After all, why not use price control as an instrument for resource allocation? Governments don't like to give up tools of this kind just because some economists tell them that in the long run price control has a very negative effect on the economy.

Yet if governments keep price controls then the negative phenomena mentioned above, like the public having to queue in front of shops selling scarce products, will automatically occur. Price regulation cannot but create a black market to meet the needs of suppliers and consumers to sell and purchase. Sometimes price control stimulates corruption and crime, when those managing the price system give preference to their acquaintances or sell merchandise to the black market operators. The black markets' product prices are far from fair. They are always higher than these prices would be if price control did not exist. Price control can even cause panic buying when there are rumors of a planned price increase.

One very commonly used price control is the rent control (on dwellings) imposed in many cities in the world. Usually, like every price control, the rent control starts at times of crisis, but once widespread it becomes hard to reverse and inhibits investment in reconstruction and building. If you happen to visit a major city in the west and find that the apartment buildings in the very center of town are dilapidated and neglected, don't be surprised. This is because the landlords do not want to invest in buildings in their ownership when rents have been frozen below the market price level.

When a government finally realizes that the distortion caused by price controls has crippled the economy to the point of causing public unrest, it usually tries to cope with the problem by using an instrument called Rationing. Rationing is supposed to ensure the access of all the population to supply of its basic needs, such as food, clothing, medication etc. The government usually imposes rationing by distributing coupons evenly among the population. Regardless of how much of a rationed product an individual wants, and how much he can afford financially, he can purchase only an amount corresponding to the amount of coupons that he has been allocated. When purchasing the rationed products he has to pay for it with the coupons as well as money.

Rationing cannot, however, solve the problem of product scarcity. Price control means that prices are fixed below the equilibrium product price. The consequence is that the supplier is not motivated to increase his production quotas, while on the other hand the consumer feels that the product price does not reflect its scarcity, or to put it more simply that the product is too cheap, and so demand for the product increases.

Price distortion caused by price control sometimes causes very surreal situations. Bread is the basic product most often subject to price control. In one country with extreme price control the price of bread was even lower than the price of corn. Government statistics showed that bread consumption rose steeply, to the point of exceeding several kilos per capita per day for the whole population. A survey initiated by government officials then discovered, that the dairy and meat-producing farmers were feeding their livestock bread rather than corn.

The policy of price control ultimately always leads to drastic price correction, and this causes further disruption in the price system in the form of high and uncontrollable Inflation. There is an old Chinese saying which probably offers the best advice on how to prevent all this mess: "Do not jump on the tiger's back until you have a plan about how to jump off it".

Sometimes price control may be the right decision, so long as the basic product supply distortion is temporary and disappears as fast as it appeared. In most cases, however, this is not the case, and the supply distortion may even be a long-term phenomenon with an upward trend. Then price control forces the government to cover the gap between the real price of the basic product and the price for which it is eventually sold. This price gap will become part of government expenses and most probably will add to the government deficit.

Yet a government deficit means an increased volume of money in circulation. If price control seems necessary, this means that the economy is already suffering from a situation of limited production capacities. We know that if an increase of volume of money in circulation happens at times of limited production capacities, then it will most likely create inflation. Inflation on the other hand will further increase the gap between the equilibrium price of the subsidized product and its price as regulated by government.

And the spiral starts to turn again as price control brings additional government expenses and deficit, which in turn cause increase in the inflation rate, which in turn widens the gap between the regulated prices and the equilibrium prices, and the carousel turns round again and again. As it turns faster and faster, the riders on the carousel rise higher and higher. Eventually out of desperation the government may decide to cut the subsidies altogether and cause a steep rise in the previously regulated Product prices. But usually this is too late, because the carousel now has its own momentum, and sudden disconnection from the power source (the price fixing) may well cause catastrophic collapse.

Yet partial controlled price increases are not effective either, because they have to be continually repeated. If an economy finds itself in this spiral of inflation and price subsidies, it is hard to find an exit from it without external impulse or aid. Such an external impulse might take the form of a sudden collapse of raw material price that influences the production cost of the basic product with the controlled price, or some other development that changes the relative prices in a way beneficial for the economy.

In view of all the problems created by price controls, we have to ask why on earth they are ever imposed and sometimes maintained for so long. Sometimes there is some justification for a price regulation policy. One is the need to correct price distortion caused by a situation in which there are too few suppliers of a certain basic product, and no alternative, and these suppliers tend to coordinate their prices instead of competing for the favor of the consumer. In extreme cases, there is only one supplier. In this case the sole producer may raise the product price to unjustified levels and may even reduce the product quality without changing its price. In such situations government control and intervention in product prices is necessary.

Again and again we witness the apparent miracle of how a floating price system perfectly ensures the availability of products for the consumer, with no need for queues and black markets. All this happens in the context of relative price stability, as compared to the steep and sudden price increases in economies with strict price control and regulation. You may well ask why it is that such a prosaic factor as product price, if loosened and freely floating, so miraculously solves all the problems that defeat centrally managed economies? The explanation is the prompt reaction of consumers and suppliers to changes in the price of the product. Every increase in the product price causes a decrease in demand for the product, while motivating suppliers to produce more of the product and try to sell it. Likewise, when the product price falls the opposite happens: consumer demand rises and supply diminishes. I like to call this phenomenon "the scissors effect of price change".

The explanation for this miracle of the price mechanism seems to me rather prosaic and can be easily explained using the following example:

Let us say a consumer plans to purchase 1 kg apples for 5 dollars, remembering that this was the price of apples when he visited the grocery shop the last time. But then in the shop he finds out that the price of apples has doubled since the last time and now 1 kg apples costs 10 dollars . Yet he still has only 5 dollars in his pocket. His most probable reaction will be to purchase half a kilo of apples and not 1 kg as usual, or else to buy pears instead of apples. Either decision will decrease the demand for apples.

On the other hand the suppliers, who last time sold 1 kg apples for 5 dollars, and made just 1 dollar profit (assuming that the production costs are 4 dollars), now suddenly see they can sell 1 kg of apples for 10 dollars and make 6 dollars profit, and so they will immediately try to increase the supply of the apples on the market, and even double the wages of the apple pickers just to bring more of the goods to the shop. After all, for a very marginal additional cost (let's assume one dollar extra cost for each kg of apples) a supplier can substantially increase his apple supply to the market, while enjoying a profit of 5 dollars for each kg of apple.

Then, however, apple production costs increase with the further increased need to satisfy the demand, and as the supply of apples to the market increases the scarcity of apples on the market is reduced, and with it the price that consumers are ready to pay. And so it goes round and round, again and again, with price decrease and increase, until the consumers and the suppliers find the perfect apple price at which all the apples picked can be sold and all the consumers will get exactly the amount of apples they want. Economists like to call this price the Equilibrium Price.

Once reached, is the equilibrium price stable and unchangeable? Not at all. It remains stable only until some of the parameters determining the product price change. What parameters? One obvious one is the income of the population (a change in the amount of money in circulation). But there could also be a change in consumers' taste and preferences and many other factors influencing the demand for products. On the other side there could be changes in supply caused by an advance in technology creating new improved or substitute products, improvement in production efficiency, the appearance of a new supplier on the market or the disappearance of an old one, or changes to some attribute of the product that mean it is perceived by market participants as a different product.

Oddly enough, time can also be one of the parameters influencing the equilibrium price of a product. Let's take as an example freshly picked fruits like blueberries, brought to the market early in the morning when they are still fresh, in the knowledge that by the evening they will be starting to decay and so lose value. As the hands of the clock advance, the price of blueberries drops. A product with great time sensitivity is a product with a short shelf-life. They include not only fresh food products that are highly perishable and so time-sensitive, but also products highly sensitive to change in fashion, like women's clothing, or products sensitive to technological changes, like mobile phones or plastic soda bottles. You will now understand that some changes in the equilibrium price occur in the very short term (from the morning to the evening in the case of blueberries), while others in the much longer term (until a new technology is developed, or consumers change their preferences). The shelf-life of products is one of the major problems in commerce. Not surprisingly, great efforts are made to develop products with long shelf-life, often at the expense of their quality. One very good example is the genetically modified tomato. It's shelf-life has been substantially prolonged, but it has lost that fine juicy taste.

If the equilibrium price changes so often, whenever one of the parameters influencing it changes, what meaning does the equilibrium price really have? Why use the concept at all and not just speak of prices changing without introducing the complicating idea of an equilibrium price? The reason is that the equilibrium price is as it were focus of attraction to which actual product prices have a tendency to move. If this focus of attraction shifts, prices are dragged towards it.

In the previous example of the apple, the price jumped to 10 dollars per kg., causing an increase of supply until the price stabilized again at (let us say) an equilibrium price of 6 dollars per kg. But then a new scientific report proves that the pear not only contains the same vitamins as apple but is also a good natural substitute to Viagra. When the report is publicized, the taste preferences of most of the men in the world will change; they switch from eating apples to eating pears and a new equilibrium price emerges for the apple. This new equilibrium remains until a new verified scientific report proves that radish mixed with apple is an even better Viagra substitute.

To show you the importance of the equilibrium price, I would like to use the image of a rudderless ship in a storm - a ship which is not completely adrift but has cast anchor in the ocean floor. Instead of being firmly fixed in the ocean floor, however, the anchor is itself shifted around by currents at the bottom. The ship, representing the product price, is swirling around the long line of the anchor in the storm, but the anchor, representing the equilibrium price, is also dragged from one place to another hundreds of kilometers away. Let us assume you are in the rescue team and you get two charts. One tracks the movement of the ship round the anchor, but the other the movement of the anchor. Which do you think will be more helpful to you in finding the location of the ship? If you want to predict the course of the product price, you should follow the equilibrium price rather than the actual price.

Can anyone be sure that this price mechanism will not collapse one day? What will happen if the basic assumptions about the price mechanism cease to be valid? What if a price increase for a product actually increases the demand for it and does not reduce it as expected? After all this is what indeed happens with jewelry, art, ancient artifacts, etc., i.e. demand for them grows as their price rises. Or what if the producers do not increase production despite the potential increase in their profits? There are many traditional societies that stand for values other than profit, like the Hippie communities in the seventies, some of them still in existence today. As far as I know they act according to different economic rules based on the slogan, "Less is more and more is less". I personally value these people but they will always be very marginal to modern societies.

Sticking with our mainstream ideology, we shall continue to work on the assumption that if the price of a product rises fewer people will want to buy it. On the other hand, when profit-driven economic carnivores and predators see their opportunity, like vultures attracted to a corpse, they too will immediately react to the higher prices with higher production supply quotas.

Not that his is the whole story. Some products have a particular price=sensitivity to sudden change in demand and supply. These are known as "price-sensitive products", and their prices react particularly dramatically to change in production quotas or consumer demand. If these products are suddenly in much greater supply for some external reason, it leads to major and immediate price change. These are mostly basic products necessary to life and the demand for them is stable. Other cases of product price-sensitivity arise where the quantity of products produced is relatively inflexible and cannot be rapidly and easily adjusted to change in demand. The reason might be the technical demands of production or else its dependence on a limited resource, which could be a scarce raw material, but could also be a high and too expensive capital requirement or entrepreneurial initiative.

On the other hand there are "price-resistant products" which react in the opposite way in the sense of being relatively insensitive in their price to changes in demand or the quotas of production and supply. These are products that can easily be replaced by an alternative Product.

The very best example of a price-resistant product is smelly French cheese, as compared to petrol for your car.

If you are fond of French cheese and are used to buying 100 grams for 10 dollars each day, what do you do when one day you find that your favorite French cheese is out of stock in the supermarket? Most probably you buy Dutch cheese for 5 dollars and moan to your friends that your much-loved delicacy is unavailable. If you are an enterprising type, then in order to substitute for the special odor of the French cheese you miss so much you will spend the remaining money on some fresh substitute garlic, and will not run around the city to find the French cheese in some other overpriced delicatessen for 20 dollars.

On the other hand, if filling up your car tank suddenly costs 100 dollars and not the 50 dollars you were used to, you won't remove your car's engine and try running it on perfume. Maybe next time you will buy a car with less demanding engine, but it will not be tomorrow.

The conclusion is that the French cheese is a "price-resistant product", while fuel is a "price-sensitive Product". This example shows the different price elasticity of different products, and the major variable influencing the level of elasticity of the product price is the existence (or not) of a substitute product. There are many alternatives (substitutes) for French cheese, even if their tastes are different, which is why its shortage on the shop shelves does not create an immediate and steep price increase (don't forget, its taste and odor improves with the time spent on the shelf). By contrast, there is no alternative to the fuel for your car; If your car uses diesel fuel, you can't use ordinary petrol.

And here we arrive at a conclusion about another basic behavioral attribute of the product price; If there is no alternative product that can easily substitute for the original one, or it takes a long time to increase or decrease the production volume of the product, any change in demand and supply will bring fast and dramatic price changes. On the other hand, if there is an alternative product that can easily substitute for the original product, the product price reactivity to changes in purchaser-supplier relations will be slow and lazy. As we already said at the beginning of this book, Product is lazy compared to Money, but not all products are equally lazy. Some products are lazier than others.

Now you have got through the first eight, "very important" chapters of this book without giving up out of boredom and consigning it to the bottom of the bookcase, I can assume you understand the deep significance of the question, "Which comes first, the Money or the Product?". Therefore, I can now move on to write about Money and one of its interesting attributes, which is that "The value of money changes as it moves along the axis of time". To say this is not to repeat what we have already described, which is that the money in your wallet or bank account may become less valuable or more valuable over time as a result of Inflation or Deflation. It means that the value of money changes according to its allocation to present or future use. The tool that moves money and its value along the axis of time is called credit.

Credit, if it is in form of money, is about borrowing and giving loans. Even if the tool for measuring the cost of the credit is money, credit may take many other forms and not all of them are necessarily about simply transferring money from a lender to a borrower and back again. Credit can be merchandise you purchased for delayed payments, with a fixed repayment schedule. Of course the loan from your bank, the mortgage on your house, or postponed payments on your credit card are all Credit.

A loan is money borrowed today with a promise of repayment. It is a tool for allocating money now from a lender to a borrower who agrees to repay it in the future. The bank is the most common mediator between creditors and debtors. Before approving a new loan the bank verifies the future feasibility of the loan repayment, either on the basis of the expected increase of the borrower's future income that will outcome of the loan given for the investment, or on the basis of the expected future income of the borrower assumed on the basis of his past income performance.

Money in your hand, ready for immediately use now, has a very different value from money expected to be earned in the future. The main reason for the difference in the value of the money on different points of the time scale is the risk associated with any expectation of future income. Even the best assured future income includes a certain element of risk. Loan defaults happen for internal reasons such as the entrepreneur's miscalculation or his limited capability, or external reasons such as a sudden change in the economy which has an impact on the enterprise. Both will mean that the banks will have to write off the debts from their assets as bad debts.

To give you a clearer understanding of how time factors affect the value of money, I will tell you a simple story, which did not happen but might well have happened. Johnny Now, who is 13 years old, has 5 dollars in his pocket that he has just received from his Mum today – it is the same sum he always receives at the beginning of every month. His friend Bobby Later, who is the same age, has no dollars in his pocket, but his mum has promised him that for his good behavior last month he will get 10 dollars at the beginning of the next month. They are both hungry and thirsty. A Big Mac with Pepsi costs exactly 5 dollars and could satisfy their hunger and thirst if they share it half & half, and even add a little to their prospects of obesity.

The question is: Who is better off, Johnny or Bobby? That depends. If Bobby Later is very hungry, he will probably promise Johnny Now all the 10 dollars he is going to receive next month just to get half of Johnny's Big Mac straightaway. If he is just moderately hungry he will give less than that and probably the two boys will compromise on 5 of Bobby's future dollars for a half of the Big Mac and Pepsi now, and they will both think it's a fair deal and their friendship will continue.

My feeling is that this compromise seems just right. Don't you feel the same? If not don't worry, it's not wrong to feel differently. It just means that your "Personal Propensity for Savings" is different from mine. But we shall come to that later.

But whatever your preference, you will agree with me that Johnny Now has a right to ask for more than 2.5 dollars for a half of his Big Mac, unless you are an altruist, which most people are not. By the way, if they agreed on the repayment of the 5 dollars within a month, in economic language we could define it as a credit transaction by which Johnny loaned Bobby 2.5 dollars for a month and charged a 100% interest rate on it.

Let me calculate 100% for a month: if Bobby fails to return the 5 dollars to Johnny because he needs the 10 dollars for a new play station 4 game, after a month his debt will grow to 10 dollars and the next month 20 dollars. To translate this into annual terms, Johnny is charging Bobby 204700% interest rate that means that after a whole year Bobby will owe Johnny 10,035 dollars. This teaches us that Johnny has made a very good deal. As for Bobby, he has made a good deal too in the sense of learning that hunger is not a very good financial adviser, and hopefully next time he will make a financial transaction with a full belly. Johnny on the other hand can only regret that he didn't invite Bobby to a fancy French restaurant, which would have cost 25 dollars instead of the 5 dollars he spent on the Big Mac, since in that case Bobby would now owe him 25 dollars instead of the 5. But we know that Johnny couldn't do that since he only had 5 dollars in his pocket. This situation is called the poverty trap of the poor, which means that if you have very little or no money, it is hard to make more money even if you happen to come across a very good business opportunity. We can also learn from the kids' behavior why the poorest people usually pay the highest interest rates.

Speaking of interest, if you have not yet understood what it is all about, it is the price the debtor pays to the lender for the service of borrowing Money from him for an exactly specified period of time. In other words the interest rate is the price paid for borrowing money. If we define it in this way, we can say that the act of giving credit is a product (service), and like any other product it has its price. This is the reason why when a loan is made an additional sum is required in addition to the repayment of the principal (the original sum loaned), and this additional sum is interest.

Like products, money when loaned has different prices depending on the difference in the brand labels of the debtor. This brand label is called credibility. The difference in interest rates charged by banks to different clients is justified by the difference in level of security the client can give the banks against the loan. This security is partly based on evidence of the value of the debtor's assets, and partly on the past performance of the debtor and his credibility.

Banks like to see figures in annual terms, and so most of the loans the banks mediate have interest rates that are easily comparable. So we know that a 5% annual interest rate is reasonable and so is 6% but that 20% is too high. Unlike the banks, who define the interest rate they charge in annual terms, there are others who like to define it on a shorter -term basis, like the credit card companies that like to charge interest on a monthly basis. Try to figure out if 1.5% monthly interest rate is low or not! By the way it works out at a 20% annual rate and not 18%, as some people might guess.

The highest interest rate I have ever paid was on police tickets for unlawful parking. These penalty fees tend to double their value every time you get a notice and don't pay up immediately. The interest rate of the police is closer to the interest rate on the loan Johnny gave to Bobby than to the banks' interest rate. Another institution accustomed to applying loan - sharking credit policy is the tax authority. If you don't want to go bankrupt, don't try to avoid or postpone tax payments. I have some useful advice to you altogether: beware of lenders who offer you loans with monthly or - even worse - weekly interest rates!

Why do we need credit and why on earth do people incur debts with all this nuisance of being forced to keep on paying up every month for most of their lives? Why can't we just keep our purchases and outgoings within the limits of our financial capacity? There are many good reasons why not. In the past a very common reason for taking loans was to buy food to feed yourself and your family.

In modern societies very few people have a problem feeding their families, yet there are many people who take loans to meet some other consumption needs, like buying a new car, credit taken with credit card to pay in the supermarket, etc. In a way these loans are all similar in that they finance consumption now and bring no potential increase of income in the future. I would put them in the same category as the loans people used to take to save their families in times of famine.

Yet as we said before, hunger is not the best reason to take loans. You will eat the money someone lent to you, rather than using it to create any activity to increase your future income and so help with the loan repayment. If the money borrowed is not used to generate additional income, but is used to increase consumption and so is "eaten up", on repayment day the borrower may find himself insolvent, lacking enough income to repay the debt. In ancient times there was a very straightforward solution for this situation: the debtor was enslaved and if his debt was large enough his whole family was enslaved too and that was the end of the story. In modern times there is no slavery to solve the problem, and instead bankruptcy law has been introduced. This releases the debtor from his debts and leaves him to live what seems to some people the ideal life of absolute freedom, free of assets and liabilities.

In short, we distinguish between Money today from Money tomorrow, and the tool we use to bridge the gap is Credit. Wherever there is credit, interest is charged. If you ask me about the rationales for taking and giving credit, and I set aside situations of sheer hunger or the desire for immediate consumption, one very good reason is the chance credit offers you to get out of the poverty trap by enabling you to exploit a business opportunity that suddenly appears on your doorstep.

Suppose one day you come across a business opportunity with potential profits, but you don't have the money you need to invest in it. On the other hand your neighbor, while not a very initiative-taking type, is unlike you highly organized, and has been regularly saving part of his earnings. Last week when you met him on the way to the train, and you did not yet know about the business opportunity, he happened to mention that the redemption date on his savings in the bank is next month. Knowing you are an entrepreneurial type with many funny ideas, he asked you how you would invest your money if you had any.

You are used to teasing him, and so at the time you probably advised him to buy a sports car to attract the attention of the beautiful young female colleague who joins you both as usual on your commuter train.

Now you know about the business idea when you meet him next time, and when he asks you about the subject again, you jump at the opportunity, and suggest that he lends his money to you. You promise him a higher interest rate than any bank would give him. You probably also explain your business plan to him, and with your complete faith in your initiative you try to use all your charm to persuade him to invest in your plan. You may be successful. After all you have a whole hour in the train together, and all your attention will be turned on your "friend", and even the young female colleague will not distract you.

You assure him there is no way that your plan can fail, and to overcome his doubts you probably offer him not only interest on his loan but also a share of the profits. After all why not? He is the one that will take all the risks by putting his money into an as yet non -existent venture that may create profits, but could be a fiasco. If your expectations of profit are not fulfilled, and you only break even or worse, make a loss, your neighbor will have a hard time getting his money back. Probably as the train is approaching your destination, you will very happily agree to give him a big share of the profit, since without his money there is no opportunity.

How much interest should you pay your neighbor? The answer to this is, "It depends". If your neighbor is the only person ready to give you the loan, and your expected profit is significant, which means that probably your venture is accordingly risky, you will pay a huge interest rate and still be happy.

Like the prices of products, interest payments are also a tool for the allocation of financial resources to encourage new investments, or to boost consumption in the present at the expense of future consumption. Again, just as prices are the major stimulator of demand and supply of products, the interest rate is a major stimulator for the allocation of money away from consumption today to savings and away from savings to investments.

Surprisingly, despite being one of the most important tools for resource allocation, the idea of charging interest on loans seems repugnant to many ideologies and societies, including medieval Christianity and Islam, but also modern Communist ideology. Yet if not rewarded, why would a person who has more money than he can or wants to spend lend it to someone who needs it? Especially if the person who needs the loan has plans to invest it in an enterprise that may reward him with higher income in the future, but carries a certain risk? It seems only fair that the lender should be rewarded for help that can be crucial for starting or developing new enterprises.

In centrally managed economics, where the decisions about investments and resources allocation are made administratively, interest is not considered a useful tool. Superficially it sounds very tempting to control capital allocation by direct planning. After all, why couldn't a centrally managed committee allocate available resources better than some imaginary market, regulated by some mysterious phenomenon called "The Interest Rate"?

History shows many examples of governments failing to resist the temptation to take charge of where to invest the available resources, saved up by those who postponed immediate pleasure for the sake of secure future income. Luckily in the democratic market economy this temptation is negligible.

In the USSR, the government annulled the function of interest and centralized all decisions on investment. It eventually decided on massive allocation of resources to projects of enormous scale, with a very long-term rate of return, and often with horrendous environmental consequences. At first the system looked very efficient, because with the establishment of the new economic system many big obviously needed projects that had been postponed in the past for lack of resources could be realized. Then the Second World War broke out and the failings of the system were hidden behind the war effort, which channeled all the investments in war equipment and machinery. But when the war ended, after the rebuilding efforts and the meeting of the most obvious human needs, centrally managed investment decisions gradually turned out to be inefficient and became more and more patently wasteful and less and less beneficial for the population. In the end the centrally managed economies invested most of the available resources in huge white-elephant projects, which led to further damage rather than fulfilling the needs of the population for products.

The Soviet government tried to offset the suffering it was causing its citizens by constant promises of a great future. It depleted its energy and other raw material resources by selling them to its allies (colonies) for fixed prices much below world prices, with a devastating effect on the environment and wastage of energy usage. It created huge military and heavy industrial factories, producing everything except the products the population asked for. Even in science investment was channeled into military purposes, or to achieve a political aim like the space program. This yielded some impressive scientific results, but in the meantime the Soviet Union was still unable to create any innovations in the sphere of consumer products, and the best it could do was to try relatively unsuccessfully to copy the consumer products produced in the market economies.

The communist system of the USSR is not the only one that has denied the positive function of interest. The Christians of medieval Europe also rejected interest as an immoral tool. But then, they did not really acknowledge the needs of the present at all. Even today in Muslim countries where Muslim law is strictly implemented, people try to operate a credit system without charging interest, which is forbidden by Sharia and perceived as evil. They have even created a whole allegedly interest-free banking system called "Islamic Banking", but this tends to involve just coming up with ingenious new names for interest and interest rates, which enable them to pretend they are not using them.

Why have so many different ideologies and faiths been so hostile to such a prosaic instrument as interest charges? My answer is that the roots of these prejudices and indeed laws against loans at interest (known pejoratively as usury), all go back to medieval times, when there was no substantial economic growth, and definitely no per capita economic growth.

And here once again we come back to the question posed at the very beginning of this book: "Which comes first, the chicken or the egg?" As we said earlier, an increase in the volume of money in circulation leads to an increase in the volume of product value in circulation. And what is Economic Growth if not increase in the volume of product value in circulation in its potential or kinetic state?

In medieval times, however, to increase the volume of money in circulation you had to overcome the obstacle of the limited availability of precious metals. How could this problem be solved? The answer was kings, who were able to give orders to mint money, and if there was not enough precious metal would try to borrow it. But in medieval times, the main reason kings needed loans was to fight wars. And wars are a very bad way to create more potential volume of product value in circulation, i.e. the equivalent to the term economic growth.

In an economy where there is no increase of production capacity to create additional economic wealth, and no increase in the *volume of product value in circulation*, the average debtor logically cannot pay interest to lenders, and most loans will not be repaid. If a war is lost, (and in every war there is a losing side), there is no way to repay the loan, not to speak of the interest. And even the winning side has to grab a great deal of booty to repay such loans. The only other way to pay back all the loans is by inflation, which is in fact just another way of not repaying a loan in full.

This does not mean that individual enterprises successful enough to pay back a loan with interest cannot exist in a stagnating economy. But if most of the interest and the principal of the loans agreed in the economy are to be repaid, then some future additional income for the payment of interest has to be created. This can be done either by increasing the volume of product value in circulation, or by reduced consumption in the future. But we are speaking about medieval times, when the only luxury for most of the people was a piece of cheese dropped in wheat porridge. So it is rather hard to think of mass reduction of consumption in this context...

The continuous difficulties with debt repayments in medieval times, resulting from economic stagnation, fuelled constant resentment among borrowers, who were usually "noblemen" fighting noble wars, towards lenders, who were mostly Jews forced to engage in this risky and dangerous business of money-lending when all other ways of earning a living were denied to them. And here we have the source of the ideologies and articles of faith that rejected interest charges as immoral. These were societies whose ideal goals did not include in their agenda any support for increasing the volume of product value in circulation. If in the year 1000 in the Middle Ages the index of the world GDP or cumulative annual value of the product volume in circulation was about 35, five hundred years later it was 58, that is a 65% increase, or 1.65 times more. 500 years later it was already 41,000, that is a 70,000% increase, or 700 times more. Most of the growth happened in the last century. By the way, this economic growth has dwarfed the growth in population that took place over the same time period. The world population grew very little between the years 1000-1500 and, then from about 500 million to 6 milliard in the last 500 years, a roughly 12-fold growth. The enormous growth in the economy, which in our terms means growth of the annual value of the *product volume in circulation*, left enough space to redistribute this additional product value among the employees as wages, among the employers as income and profit, among the equity investors as profits and dividends, and among the bankers and bank depositors as interest on loans.

This is why in the modern market economy the charging of interest has ceased to be the object of moral disapproval and is a practice considered wholly respectable and engaged in by reputable and very influential banks. It is also why when an economy is based on credit, for which interest is charged, it needs to grow continuously. Incidentally, the need for growth applies to all the participants who are used to enjoying a share of the increased added volume of product value. In a modern economy, whenever the economy ceases to grow it means that the banks will have mounting problems getting repayment of the loans they gave to the borrowers, not to speak of the interest they charge on them, unless someone else among the employees, employers, depositors, investors, gives up his share of the product cake.

If the credit-based private economy needs continuous economic growth to secure financial stability, governments need increased tax collection which can be secured in the long run only by the increased tax base of the private sector. And here you have the basis all over the world for the comprehensive support for economic policy encouraging continuous economic growth. Most economists, bankers, politicians and other economic leaders are even afraid to ask publicly the question - "Is this economic growth ultimately beneficial for the people?" Maybe the price of this economic growth, in the form of destruction of the natural environment, inevitable uneven distribution of the wealth, etc. is higher than the benefit of such continuous economic growth? (Do you remember the short blanket? There is no free lunch in the economy.) It seems as if today, given the existing economic financial system, an economy with zero-growth is not a relevant political or economic option.

This also means that if for some reason the politicians after all decide to freeze further economic growth, the whole financial and bank system will have to be changed. (Maybe Islamic Banking is not such a bad idea after all).

Loans and debts are the main reasons for the liquidation of enterprises. If not for loans there would be no reason for bankruptcy. You may well ask here why so many people take the risk of losing everything, and why they can't just limit themselves and their activities to the amount of capital they possess? There are several reasons, and the first is the entrepreneur syndrome, which is related to the adventure syndrome, meaning people who strongly believe that if they have money they will be able to make more of it. Then more and more money, and all this out of the strange belief that it will make them happy.

Yet not all ideas invested in potential future income are secure. I recollect a friend of mine, who as a child used to run around the dining room with his arms spread out making strange noises BRRR, BRR, BRR until his mother shushed him. When he grew up he decided to realize his childhood dream and open a new shop selling airplane model kits. Later on he was forced to learn the bankruptcy law.

But then another entrepreneur friend of mine bought an old factory in a very busy neighborhood. At first I wondered what he was up to, but he converted the factory into an apartment house. Then he sold the apartments and bought a new factory, and another one, and another one, until he owned a skyscraper in 5 Avenue Manhattan New York. Every time I met him, he would never stop complaining about what a trial it was to own so much property and have so little cash. Yet there is nothing wrong with giving loans to this friend of mine, whose obsession is to make residential houses out of factories, and factories out of residential houses. Basically if you ignore his boring complaints about his lack of cash, and continuous talk of who pays him more and who less, he is a quite nice guy.

Savings and Investments are two opposite sides of the same coin. They are the phenomena that allocate product consumption from today to the future. Some historians say that savings started at a very early stage of the human history, when the first human communities changed from hunters-gatherers to agrarians and needed to save some of the grain produced in one season for the next sowing season. And probably already then, some individuals in times of hunger lost their patience and ate the saved grain, and when there were no more saved seeds, they had to turn to their neighbors for loans to survive.

The invention of credit cards, and then consumer credits, and individual overdrafts had much in common with the premature eating of saved grain. They channeled more and more finance into consumption and less and less to investments. The bankers were happy with this arrangement, since it saved them the bother of having to read and try to understand complicated business plans, which are even more boring than this book. All the banks needed was a wage payroll, or tax payment statement and they could calculate how much out of your income you could pay to the bank until you were expected to retire, and on this basis give you loans. By giving many loans of small amounts the bank does not have to worry that some big debtor will go bankrupt. If a small client goes bankrupt, because he lost his job, or played the slot machines too much on his vacation in Las Vegas, it will be insignificant for the bank as whole. Yet this arrangement, instead of channeling financial resources into investment in future potential production capacity of some economic added volume, is used for immediate consumption.

The mortgage is a different form of loan. It is connected to the ownership of a property, which secures the loan as collateral. This guarantee by property, which is a long-term assurance of repayment, opened up the way for very long-term loans, sometimes lasting an entire lifetime. These long-term loans made almost everybody a property owner.

But what happened next was a far more dangerous and potentially devastating process initiated by the banks themselves. You are living happily in a cottage in a suburb paying monthly rent to the landlord, when one day you are approached by a bank agent, who asks "Why don't you take a loan to purchase your house? Instead of paying rent to the landlord, you will make a similar payment to the bank, and the house will eventually be yours.

All you have to do is to find your own 10% of the house price, and the credit agent will immediately show you nice graphs, showing you how much money you are going to make as the home price of your property goes up. The next year the agent turns up again and tells you how, exactly as he predicted, your house price has gone up, and how you have in fact earned more "money" from the appreciation of your house price than from your work. He invites you to his office, and offers you an additional loan against this extra value of your house. If you ask what you need this extra money for, he will answer unhesitatingly, - here I have a nice brochure for a nice vacation in Las Vegas.

In Las Vegas unfortunately you lose on the slot machine...... But don't worry about the slot machine, since even if you lose the loaned money, next year the agent will turn up again and give you another loan, since every year your house price goes up.

It is not at all surprising that your house price has increased, when the same and many other agents like yours have been giving more and more loans to more and more house owners. This process not only increases the volume of money in circulation, but channels this additional money into the house market, causing the specific phenomenon of skyrocketing house prices, or what people like to called a bubble.

This process may continue until someone says to himself, "I've had enough of all these vacations in Las Vegas, where anyway I only lose money on the boring gambling machines", and so decides not to take out a new loan. Suddenly there is less volume of money in circulation in the house market. If many people are equally fed up with this continuous routine of new loans, and new vacations, and so follow him, house prices will stagnate and there will be no demand for additional mortgages, and no more new money added to circulation in the housing market.

Then someone decides to sell his house, and asks the same price that his neighbor got for a similar house last year, plus some small addition of course. But he very soon discovers that nobody is ready to buy it for last year's price, or even less. And suddenly the houses prices stop growing and even start to drop. But the real problem starts when the bank discovers that house prices are below the level of the loans they gave last year on houses. At this point the banks, which up to now have been causing the house price boom with their mortgage loans, help to create a house price collapse by a new strict lending policy.

Although it is often not obvious which came first, an economic slowdown or a credit squeeze, it seems that they mutually influence each other in the same direction. This is again what I would call the phenomenon of closing scissors, since if the economy ceases to grow, the volume of money in circulation ought to be increased to reignite growth, but here what happens is the very opposite.

10. Banks and the Great Money-Printing Machine, or where has all the Money gone?

Writing this chapter about the Central Bank and the commercial banks, I can't help thinking of Liza Minnelli singing "Money, Money, Money" in the film Cabaret.

Yes, if you ask me why we need all these banks, my answer would probably be MONEY, MONEY, MONEY!

I wonder sometimes where Money gets its strange sex-appeal. Apart from attraction to the other gender, there is probably nothing else that stirs such intense feelings. Some people love money, others hate it and dream of a world without it, but no one is indifferent to it. I am always rather amazed whenever I enter a shop offering a product, whether goods or services, to think the shop will readily accept a bit of paper with a rather dull picture on it in exchange for any Product I choose to purchase.

It never fails: when I enter a shop, the same scenario always works. And it works in spite of the fact that there is no real value behind the money I am handing over. If the shopkeeper bothered to inquire at all, he would soon find out that this money is not really backed by gold, diamonds or any other "valuable thing". He would realize that the only reason the money has any value is because it is just his experience that whenever he enters the shop next door to purchase a shirt, or whatever he needs, he can pay for it with the same paper money he received for the product he sold.

How come this all works? The answer is faith, and if you think of yourself as a rational atheist who believes in nothing unless he has real evidence for its existence, then you shouldn't be giving or accepting money. Money is all about faith in Money, trust that it represents a certain value exchangeable for Product, regardless of whether the pictures on the bank notes are funny, inspiring or just anachronistic, or whether like dollars they carry the legend, "IN GOD WE TRUST". To be honest, I would probably have "IN PAPER WE TRUST" printed on dollar bills. This value attributed to paper Money is just a myth that is accepted by everyone, on the same level as some people accept the existence of UFOs.

If we want to talk about how this faith in Money has been created, we need to talk about banks, which are after all the main institutions holding and operating your money. But before I get to banks I would like to tell you about a conversation I had with my uncle, who lived his whole adult life in communist Slovakia. I saw him for the first time in twenty years when I visited Slovakia after the fall of the communist regime. We spoke a lot about the past, but at one point I tried to show off a little, and told him that I had just sold some company shares and made a profit out of it. He stared at me incredulously, unable to understand what I was talking about. After I gave him a long explanation, to which he listened attentively, he made just one comment, "Luftgesheft" ["air business" in Yiddish].

The first step to understanding all this is to ask what happens when you take 1000 dollars to a commercial bank to deposit it there, so it will be safe in the vault and you will be able to forget the worries you had when it was still in your wallet and you knew you could lose it or someone could steal it off you. Your feeling of trust and security will increase when you are welcomed in to the bank building, with its huge hall, shiny clean big windows, padded seating and nice - looking young clerks running around you. If you deposit more than an average monthly wage you will even be offered a glass of water or tea, and they will promise you interest on your deposits.

But when I tell you what the bankers really do with your money, you may not feel so calm and relaxed anymore!

The banks can generously pay you interest and even refrain from charging you maintenance costs for keeping your money in their vault, because they are making profit out of lending your money to someone else at a higher interest rate than you get on your deposit.

The borrower, who gets a loan of your money from the bank, is no keener than you are to carry his money around in his wallet, and so he too deposits it in a bank vault - not necessarily the vault in your bank, but it doesn't matter which bank vault because the effect will be the same. Even if the borrower needs the loan for some immediate payment, he will most probably transfer the loaned money to the bank account of the supplier that he needs to pay, and this supplier also likes to keep his money in a bank vault. So in fact the money almost never leaves the bank vault unless someone withdraws it from a cash machine or from the cashier and puts it in his pocket or wallet. Could it be true that the banks deliberately limit the amount of cash available to the cashiers in their safes so as to discourage you from taking your money out as cash? Oh perish the thought! However, in some banks, if the depositor wants to withdraw a larger amount of cash out of the bank vault, he has to notify the bank of his intention a day or two in advance. And have you noticed that people wanting to make withdrawals almost always have to wait in a queue in banks? In practice the most frequent way to withdraw cash money these days is to use a cash machine, where the money available for withdrawal is limited to relatively small amounts.

If you have to make large payments, you probably do it with a check, credit card or internet banking. None of these forms of payment requires the bank to open its vault doors.

Now you can see that your miserable ten 100-dollar bills, which you intended to have the bank keep in a very secure place, have in turn been deposited in an account belonging to some other borrower unknown to you.

The banks know a lot about money on deposit, and so are confident that not all the depositors of the cash money in the bank vault will come to the bank at the same moment to take out all their deposits in cash. (If the worst comes to the worst, they can put a note on the cash machine saying, "No cash available", or "Sorry due to technical problems your card has been swallowed" and everything will look innocent).

Since the bank is making its profits from loans and not from deposits, it will try to loan as much of the deposits as "credible borrowers" can be found for.

We have said earlier that money deposited in bank vaults will only change its status from potential to kinetic if it is asked for and given as credit. But of course the banks do not give credit just like that. They charge interest for it.

What is more, the creation of loans out of money available in the bank is not automatic. An actual demand for the potential credit has to come from somewhere and someone. The bank also has to agree to this demand for credit and give the loan to the potential borrower. Only the actual lending of the money will change the status of money from potential to kinetic, thus increasing the volume of money in circulation.

The rate of interest will ultimately decide how much credit will be asked for. If the interest rate is too high, the demand for credit will be low, and so the volume of money in circulation will be low. This direct connection between demand for credit and the interest rate is easily explicable when the loans are for investment in new business ventures. The business venture might be a production plant, but also shop or merchandize stock, or any other activity expected to bring a future return that it is hoped will be higher than the investment itself.

If there are enough credit-worthy borrowers, then theoretically the bank system could give an unlimited volume of loans without the need to open the bank vault at all. In reality, depositors aware of the "Luftgesheft" status of the money on which the bank system is based may suddenly decide (whether for good or mistaken reasons) that their money is no longer safe in the bank vault, and so will ask to withdraw all their deposits. When other depositors see this happening, they may do the same, and suddenly a queue of nervous and unsatisfied depositors appears in front of the bank doors, which will most probably be locked. The people run around in panic, hoping to be able to save some fraction of the money they deposited to the bank vault.

To take a closer look at what Money is all about, I shall start from a definition like: Money is a perfect tool to give value to Products. Money can be easily transferred from one owner to another, and from immediate usage to postponed usage. Money can be kept in a bank vault, but a wallet is as good as a bank for small amounts, and for large amounts the mattress will also do, since Money isn't something that will "go off" unless you keep in a refrigerator or a special storage facility, and you don't need staff to maintain it. And if Money is properly deposited in some yield- producing investment, or in some person's enterprise, you will see it propagate over time.

Money has a well-defined price, which is the interest rate and can be relatively easily manipulated. *The volume of money in circulation* is relatively easily increased and decreased. Money can be accumulated easily. If deposited in the bank it can generate a steady income. If you decide to keep it under the mattress, it will still hold its nominal value very well and so long as there is no inflation even its real value will be unaffected, and you will be able to purchase the same volume of products with it in the future as you could now.

The most important attribute of Money, however, is that it has to be scarce! If it becomes too abundant, it loses its value and all the functional properties I have just mentioned. Consider the difference between silicon crystal and diamond: silicon crystal is so abundant that it is almost worthless – costing no more than a handful of sand. Diamonds on the other hand are very expensive and highly valued just because they are scarce, even though they are crystals like silicon, and the two are very much alike, so only an expert (unluckily for men most women are this kind of expert) can tell the difference between them.

In the past, kings, dictators and other scoundrels were all very aware that Money had to be scarce, and so they created Money out of precious metal, which is hard to find and expensive to extract from Mother Earth. Then they monopolized the gold and silver mines and the minting of coin. To make sure that no fraud occurred, real or suspected adulteration of the coins was severely punished. In lesser cases you could lose your hands, and in severe cases you could lose your head...

The practice of using a coinage based on actual gold or other precious metals as a payment tool, which applied for most of human history, worked quite well despite usually causing a situation in which there was less *volume of money in circulation* than potential volume of product value in circulation. It also meant that the *volume of product value in circulation* per capita, and average personal wealth, stayed more or less stable. Any changes in the *volume of product value* in circulation were marginal, and if they occurred were relatively easily equalized by gradual price changes of the products or by change in the *volume of money in circulation*. The most common reason for change in per capita wealth and production capacity was sudden major population change, caused by outbreaks of plague or some other natural or manmade disaster.

The most disastrous plague in European history was the Black Death epidemic in the 14th century, when one third of the European population perished. Most economic historians agree that this sudden dramatic drop in the population brought substantial change in the economic circumstances, and later the economic behavior, of Europeans. The change in economic behavior following the Black Death is usually related to wage increase caused by the sudden shortage of field workers. The pandemic had depleted the labor force, and there were not enough field workers to cultivate the available arable land, which remained at pre-plague size, and so the bargaining power of the peasantry increased. But the land was not the only resource, the plague had not reduced. Other resources like crop seeds, horses, domestic animals, but also the volume of money in circulation, were likewise not touched by the plague. So in contrast to the era before the Black Death, the volume of money in circulation after the plague exceeded the volume of the product value in circulation. In the wake of the Black Death it seems this gave rise to a situation that we define in this book as "Money comes first". It was probably one if the triggers for the period of economic growth that was to end the epoch of the Middle Ages and initiate the new age of the Renaissance in Europe.

There came a day when someone decided that gold money was uncomfortable and unsafe to carry about in pockets or pouches. Gold money was heavy, it could get worn or battered, and could attract robbery. So that someone deposited the gold in the vault of the richest and the most trustworthy merchant in the town, and the merchant gave him a note of demand, which entitled him to pick up the gold again whenever he needed it. Later, the depositor needed to purchase some merchandise from a vendor, but being too lazy to go back to get his gold from the merchant, he just gave the vendor his note of demand and told him to go and pick up the gold from the merchant's vault for himself.

All this was possible because the purchaser and the vendor both knew the merchant to be trustworthy and were confident that he would hand over the gold when the note was presented. But the vendor himself was a lazy type, and when he needed to pay another supplier, instead of going to the merchant to pick up the gold, he again just transferred the note of demand to the supplier. End of story: there was no need to touch the gold in the merchant's vault at all.

Starting with this discovery, the whole monetary system was built up on people's faith that the gold holder or the Money Reserve holder would not refuse to come up with the value of the bank notes on demand. To achieve trust between people who did not actually know each other, the government and the banks came up with the story that the notes of demand that they printed, (bank notes) represented a certain value of gold bullion, with a fixed price, which could always be withdrawn on demand by any holder of the notes. Any lack of belief in this story, or distrust of the system, would of course cause the collapse of the economy. To prevent a collapse like this, governments kept emphasizing to the public that they were very secure, trustworthy gold depositors who can be relied upon to keep Money scarce. To make Money seem even more trustworthy, kings and rulers had their portraits printed on the bills. Even in a republic without a king like the United States, governments tend to print portraits of their presidents or other confidence-inspiring national figures on their paper money. The only important banknote that has no portrait on it is the Euro. Guess why?

To support this story of paper Money, the system artificially fixed the gold price at a high level, and whenever a new gold deposit was found, people went crazy. Have you ever heard about the California gold rush? It turned whole societies upside-down, leading people to endanger their own lives and their whole families just to strike a golden vein.

To give credibility to the government story, for centuries gold was expensively and laboriously excavated out of the deepest mine shafts ever dug, and then reburied again in the form of gold bullion in the depths of the bank vaults. This whole irrational system was created to make sure people believed that behind their bank note there was enough gold to be returned on demand for a fixed and unchangeable price. This madness prevailed until the early 1970s, but even today you will find some very influential people who, whenever the economic system is in crisis, insist that the reason is that it is no longer based on gold. They cling to this notion, despite the obvious fact that in the times when gold was still proclaimed the basis of the bank notes and the government was liable to exchange bank notes for equivalent gold, if all the depositors of gold in the bank, (the holders of bank notes) had come in on the same day to demand their share of the gold, the gold-based Money System would still have collapsed immediately.

Anyway, it finally dawned on people that it was very arbitrary to fix the volume of money in circulation to the value of gold, and it was better to try to fix it to what it has to represent, which is the *volume of product value in circulation* at fully employed production capacity.

But if gold is not the basis for the creation of Money then how is Money created? The answer is by government deficit. Modern governments learned from history that it was useful to hold a monopoly in Money creation, and so they have monopolized the right to print Money, and every time a government creates a deficit in its budget, it finances it by printing new Money.

How is this Money-creating deficit accomplished? As we have seen above, a government, which is by definition also one of the suppliers of products (mainly services), usually insists on supplying more than it can afford to pay from the taxes it collects. By doing so, it creates government deficit. By a complicated process this deficit eventually turns into additional new cash Money in circulation.

Of course, to keep up a show, the government does not print Money directly, but does so by issuing government debt securities. The government empowers the central bank to sell and repurchase these government debt securities on the open market.

But where does the Central Bank get the Money to repurchase the government debt securities? The answer is that it creates the Money out of nothing by printing it. So whenever the central bank repurchases the government debt securities, it adds to the volume of money in circulation, and whenever it sells the debt securities it sucks part of the volume of money out of circulation.

The main question the government constantly has to ask itself is what the limits of this game are. Up to what volume is new money in circulation beneficial to the economy and when does it start to be damaging? The answer is that it is beneficial up to the point when the volume of money in circulation is equal to the volume of product value in circulation at fully utilization of the economy. How do we measure whether the economy is fully utilized? Probably the best and the easiest indicator to follow up is the number of unemployed. Putting two and two together, at times of full employment and inflationary pressures the government should not create deficit, while at times of deflation and unemployment a government deficit is even desirable.

But let us get back to the problem of trust, and basically the maintenance of the pretense that Money has a real value? If trust disappears, the system grinds to a halt or falls through the floor. This is exactly what happened in the USA in 1907, when for some reason the depositors in the banks stopped believing in the monetary system, panicked, and stampeded to withdraw their deposits. This caused the collapse of privately-owned commercial banks, and with them the US economy. After this disaster the banks and the US federal government started to think about a federal bank system that would prevent commercial banks collapsing just because of irresponsible rumors spread out from some unknown source.

That is how the US central bank was created, and it was by no means as obvious and as smooth a step as you might imagine. In the past, before the 1907 crisis, a central bank had been created in the USA several times only to be abolished again. The Federal Reserve Bank was finally established in the USA on the eve of the First World War. When the war was over and the European countries finally found some time to attend to their economies, they followed the US example and created their own Central Banks. (Great Britain already had one).

The central bank's main task was and remains to create trust in Money, even if it is made just of paper or plastic card, and even if it is nothing more than a virtual line in the computer screen. The central bank has to make people believe that Money really represents the value it pretends to represent, or in other words that money scarcity is exactly as needed, to enable the available *volume of product value to circulate* without obstructions, and is neither more nor less.

This correct level of scarcity of money, which I would like to call the **Equilibrium Scarcity of Money**, is a precondition for the creation of a sustainable Money, or (to put it better) **Monetary System**. It is not at all easy to calculate exactly the *volume of money* needed for it to be in equilibrium with the *volume of product value in* circulation at a production rate of full employment. To get as close as possible to the equilibrium point, the central bank tries to avoid sudden and disruptive changes of its interest policy. It takes small steps, or to be more exact makes small increases or decreases in central bank interest rates, usually published once every month; then it monitors the reaction of the economy, and then decides again on the next small step. The effect of the central bank's policy is not immediate, and so only the future will show the reaction of the economy to the economic policy implemented by the central bank. There are many experts on the past, but there are no real experts on the future, and so from time to time the central bank makes mistakes. This is why central bankers sometimes seem to be so stubborn and conservative.

Having made the great discovery that Money could be created out of paper, with no need for a connection with a certain rare element, governments with their tendency to spend much more than they can collect in taxes started to create budget deficits. It was not long before the unbearable lightness of printing paper Money became apparent, and some governments printed so much of it that Money lost its most important attribute, its scarcity.

In Germany after the First World War and in some Southern American countries, governments could not resist the temptation to print more and more Money until their economies were deluged in money far in excess of the volume of product production capacity. Look what happened to the currency of such countries:

Bitter experience showed that governments were capable of reducing the value of Money to nothing more than its intrinsic value as scraps of paper, useful only for stuffing cracks and lighting fires. The people, but also governments themselves, ceased to trust the ability of governments to ensure the scarcity of Money, and so they empowered Central Banks to be the guardians of the stability of the financial system, and in all modern democratic states with a market economy the Central Bank operates with a lot of independence to defend Money even against its worst enemy, the government itself. Sometimes a central bank is even successful in opposing the tendency of the government to print more Money to finance its shopping habit.

If a psychoanalyst had the Central Bank on the couch, then he might see it as the Superego of the whole Monetary System, the disciplinary element that ensures the smooth flow of the Money in circulation that is necessary to secure the opposite side of the same coin, which is the smooth flow of the Product in circulation. The psychoanalyst would then be able to explain the Obsession of central bankers with maintaining the value of the currency, and their Neurotic overreaction to the smallest signs of an outbreak of inflation. Finally, he would be concerned with the Paranoia of the central bank, which breaks out among central bankers whenever the commercial banks are threatened by their depositors.

Fortunately, this book is not a psychoanalytical case study but a popularizing explanation of how the central bank maintains the money that it prints, holds and regulates in its value against other currencies, but that mainly it defends from Money's greatest enemy, its creator the government, which always wants to spend more than it can afford without regard to the long - term consequences of government deficit for the value of Money.

So how does a central bank actually operate? We have already said that its major operational tool to influence the *volume of money in circulation* is regulation of the price of money, in other words the interest rate.

The central bank's faith in the effectiveness of this instrument is so fundamental that it has even developed a funny mathematical formula, according to which it manipulates the interest rate to achieve an Inflation target declared by the government. Then the central bank makes a declaration of its own on the monetary policy based on the target Inflation, and waits to see what will happen. Surprisingly, in most cases the Inflation target policy works. The trouble is that nobody is sure if it works because of the objective effect of the interest rate, imposed on the monetary system by the central bank, or just because of the expectations created by the announcement of the Inflation policy, declared jointly by the government and the central bank.

The main task of the central bank is to create enough *volume of money in* circulation to correspond with the *volume of product value in circulation* at full utilization of all or at least most of the production capacity. You probably understand that the main problem of the central bank is to decide what this full-utilized production volume actually is.

Since in parallel with economic and monetary stability, full employment is the other major hot issue that interests the government, usually the major indicator for full utilization is full employment of the labor force, but sometimes resources apart from labor can also be indicators of the level of utilization of production capacity. In most cases this has to be a major resource which if in short supply and overpriced would limit production capacity. For example, it might be a basic energy source, fiscal capital availability, management capacity, or electricity production capacity. But for the sake of simplicity, let us assume that the full utilized capacity is known and predictable. Then all that is needed from the central bank is to print enough money to create a money base that will fill the commercial bank vault to a level enabling the commercial banks to circulate the right volume of money.

We have already explained that if we want to prevent inflation or deflation, or in other words if we want to keep the production capacity fully employed without causing a general price increase, the *volume of money in circulation* has to be in equilibrium with the *volume of product value in circulation*. We also know that the main tool used by the central bank to influence the *volume of money in circulation* is the interest rate.

How come the interest rate has such an impact on the economy? It is because before taking new loans to invest in a new project, the entrepreneur will carefully calculate the expected rate of return on his projected new business venture. He will then compare the potential profits of the investment with the alternative of the interest payments he could receive from a bank deposit. If the new enterprise venture looks as if it will bring a higher return than the interest rate he would have to pay on the loans, he will make the investment, but if not, he will not bother with the investment. This system of comparing the interest rate with the expected return will place the venture either in the category of "do it" or in the category of "don't do it". If the interest rate is reduced many new ventures not hitherto profitable will become profitable while if the interest rate is raised, many ventures will become unprofitable. This explains why the decision to invest or not to invest in a new business enterprise financed by a loan is directly influenced by the interest rate. We said above that money deposited in bank will change its status from potential to kinetic only if taken/given as a loan. The conclusion; the interest rate has a very strong influence on the volume of money in circulation.

As for the depositor, he too is influenced by the interest rate. If the interest on deposits in the bank rises, some potential depositors who were dithering about whether to buy a new car will probably postpone the purchase to next year so as to increase their deposit, but if interest rates fell they may well prefer to get the car now. So the potential depositor also has an eye on the interest rate, which makes him decide between the category of "deposit it" or "don't deposit it".

From this it should be clear that the interest rate is the primary tool of the central banks for influencing the volume of money in circulation. But if you think the central bank manipulates it by simple setting the interest rate for the commercial banks, you are mistaken. The interest rate is a price like any other price. If it were administratively fixed, that would constitute price control. We already know the kind of damage price controls can inflict when imposed administratively on certain products. The same would happen if price controls were imposed on money. Just imagine: if the interest rate were fixed at too low a level, there would be queues in front of loan clerks in banks just like the queues in front of shops under communism, and if the interest rate were too high, the bank halls would be empty, and the islanders would be queuing up at unemployment offices.

So instead of fixing the interest rate directly and rigidly, central banks and governments have come up with several tools to regulate the interest rate indirectly. Before using any tool to fix interest, however, the Central Banks have to decide what the right volume of money in circulation needs to be to secure price stability at full employment. To prevent over-shooting, the central bank uses the system of trial and error, squeezing or enlarging credit and the volume of money in circulation inch by inch, and carefully monitoring the eventual results. This cautious step-by-step process – or if you prefer - a constant kind of pincer tweaking, is supposed to create a balance between the volume of Money and the Product Value in as smooth a way as possible.

Have you ever asked yourself where the commercial banks or the credit card issuers get all the money to give you as overdraft credits, mortgages, credit card loans, leasing credits and so on?

Just think about it: last month you probably paid your rent or mortgage, bought some stuff in supermarkets, some clothing, petrol, a few presents, gadgets, and had lunch or dinner in a restaurant, maybe even a vacation… If you live in one of the high-income countries of Europe, Japan, the USA or other such places, you and your family probably spent a few thousand dollars in the last month. But how much cash did you actually hold in your hand? Probably just a few hundred. So how did all this money come to existence? You probably received most of it as wages, but were your wages paid in cash money or by direct transfer to your account? Then again, have you ever wondered where all the money suddenly mysteriously disappears to in times of economic crisis?

Let us go back to our island. Let us assume, there is only one bank institution in the island, so all the people and firms or organizations deposit their money in the same bank, and all the payments are done without cash. If there is no limit and no regulation on the volume of loans, the bank could theoretically give an infinite volume of loans, even on the basis of just one deposited pound. Of course this is on condition that all the loans and payments will always be deposited back in the bank, so the one pound never leaves the bank vault.

In theory, the bank could carry on this recycling of the original one pound deposit until more than one depositor turns up at the bank and asks to withdraw the one actual pound note he deposited previously in the bank. If only one of the depositors comes and asks to take out the one pound, the bank can give it to him. However, what if two depositors come to withdraw their deposits at the same moment? The bank will be in deep trouble. (It is not at all important whether the withdrawer is the original depositor of the one pound, or someone who took the loan from the bank and deposited it again in the same bank in his current account). If a second pound is demanded, the commercial bank will have no cash to repay it. When this happens, rumors start to spread among the depositors that the bank is in difficulty, and probably all the depositors will arrive demanding the money they have deposited in the bank in cash. Then probably they will find the front doors of the bank locked as we have already explained above.

As we have already emphasized, if someone deposits money in the bank, the bank doesn't necessarily put the money in the vault but will lend it to someone else. That borrower will most probably not withdraw the whole loan from the bank in cash but will put it in his current account in the bank, or use it to pay for a Product direct to the supplier's checking account. So the loan goes back into a bank account, and all that is circulating in reality is checks, credit-card debits, or changes of numbers on the computer display. So the conclusion, the original money deposited into the vault can be given as loan again and again to someone else and in principle it can circulate again and again and again.

Even if the banks are very cautious with loans, people may out of nowhere lose their trust in the bank, or even worse in the whole banking system, and panic may then prompt all the depositors to try to withdraw all their deposits from the bank vaults at the same time, even if the debtors are credible and never default on their debts, a commercial bank can easily fall into insolvency.

The conclusion is that a certain percentage of the deposit has to be kept as a reserve to cope with that eventuality, and this reserve is called the **Minimum Reserve Requirement**. But what percentage of the deposit does this minimum reserve have to represent? Is it up to each bank to decide this rate (percentage)?

For example the commercial banks in US are required to keep 10% of the deposits in reserves. If you deposit 1000 dollars in your bank account, only 90% of this very first 1000-dollar cash deposit can be given as credit. If the loan is then deposited in the bank account of the borrower, and this happens again and again, the 1000 dollars will create an accumulated credit of 9000 dollars: this 9000 dollars becomes volume of money in circulation, while 1000 dollars will remain in the bank vault. By the way, from the perspective of the bank, the money deposited by borrowers out of the first or subsequent loans is no different in quality from an original cash deposit.

So what do we have here? After you deposited your hard-earned 1000 dollars in the bank, we now have 1000 dollars in the vault and 9000 dollars money in circulation given by the banks as loans, and deposited in bank accounts. Do not be confused: the 1000 dollars not in circulation are not the original 1000 dollars you initially deposited in the bank but the 10% remaining fraction of the deposits made by you and the borrowers, assuming that 90% of these deposits were progressively recycled into new loans.

Here the Central Bank steps in, for one of its main tasks is precisely to fix a certain Minimum Reserve Requirement Rate to secure the stability of commercial banks. The Central Bank not only fixes the Minimum Reserve Requirement Rate, but demands that the commercial banks deposit it overnight in the central bank's reserve vault. If it is unable to do this, the commercial bank is heavily financially penalized. (Do not even dare to suggest that the demand that commercial banks deposit the Minimum Reserve Requirement Rate in the Central Bank's vault every night has anything to do with any distrust of commercial banks by the Central Bank!).

If the commercial banks don't have the money to fulfill the Minimum Reserve Requirement because they have given too much in loans or too many depositors withdraw their money from the vault, before the Central Bank vault closes for the night, they run all over the city to ask other commercial banks for an overnight loan to bridge the gap, (probably this is why the commercial banks headquarters are all concentrated in the "City"). If the bank needing the loan is credible in the eyes of the other commercial banks, they will usually provide that loan, for a somewhat lower interest rate than the penalty rate the Central Bank would charge the offending bank for not meeting the demanded Minimum Reserve Requirements Rate.

What happens next? If the Minimum Reserve Requirements Ratio is 10%, this means that the system enables commercial banks to give credit of up to 900 dollars out of 100 dollars deposited in the bank. This 900 dollars is the real potential volume of money in circulation. If the Minimum Reserve Requirement is raised to 20%, this would result in the reduction of the potential volume of money in circulation to only 400 dollars. It is obvious that a relatively small change in the Minimum Reserve Requirement Rate has an enormous impact on the volume of money in circulation. Theoretically the Central Bank could use this instrument to squeeze or enlarge the volume of credit volume given by the banks, and with it the volume of money in circulation, very easily indeed. In fact, because this is a very blunt instrument, the Central Bank is reluctant to use it for this purpose, and prefers to rely on tools that are more delicate.

Now we can return to the question of where money disappears to in times of economic crisis. The answer is that it does not disappear because it physically never really existed - except as credit given based on 10% of the cash originally deposited in the commercial banks. This credit is very profitable for the banks because they charge more interest on loans than they are obliged to pay on the deposits. Or at least it is very profitable so long as they don't have difficulties getting their loans repaid. To try to ensure they are paid back, the commercial banks demand collateral securities, usually some kind of asset, against the credit. By pledging assets, the borrower limits his right of ownership of the asset, and the bank then has the security that if the borrower defaults on the loan it can sell the pledged asset and cover its loss even if only partially.

Despite all the precautions taken by the banks when deciding to whom to give a loan, and careful pricing of the value of the assets that will be the collaterals securing the loans, in times of economic crisis the actual prices of the assets may fall well below the value of the loan. Without enough asset-value coverage of loans, the banks become more reluctant to give new credits and new loans, and suddenly there is less available Money in the economy. Less available Money means a further drop in the asset prices. This drop in the asset prices increases the tendency of the asset owners to sell their possessions, and this sets off a new round of price reduction of the assets. And again, the banks have a new problem with the value of the collaterals and a new round starts again.

Reduction of the volume of credit and loans also puts a squeeze on the volume of the money in circulation, and this in itself causes a drop in the volume of the product value in circulation. And here we are already in a serious spiral. The reduction of the volume of the Product value in circulation means unemployment and unemployment means difficulties for some of the debtors, mainly those who took out mortgage loans and consumer credits and lost their jobs. As you can see this process is self-perpetuating, and sometimes it can happen in a very short time.

At this point the banks are forced to erase some of the credits from their assets, and admit that they have not made a profit but on the contrary have made a loss. This reduces their capacity to give credit because the banks have to fulfill another requirement of the central bank, which is known as the Equity Requirement. To explain this issue, I must first explain the concept of equity.

Equity (share capital) is all the value (in the form of money or another form) that company owners have invested in any legal entity or company, plus all the retained earnings that the entity has accumulated in the course of its existence but not paid out to the owners as dividend, and minus all generated losses. In other words, equity represents the current market value of all the assets of a legal entity, minus the total value of all its liabilities. This excess asset value represents the company's net value, which as distinct from the owners' loans is not repayable to the investors in the normal course of business.

The Central Bank imposes on commercial banks an obligatory Minimum Equity Requirement, as a percentage of the loans the bank provides to borrowers. This requirement has an even more dramatic effect than the Minimum Reserve Rate Requirement imposed on banks. As I explained above, the bank leverages the deposits of the public up to nine times (in the US) as loans to borrowers. The equity of the bank is only a small fraction compared to the volume of the deposits in the bank and obviously an even smaller fraction relative to the total volume of credit given by the bank. Therefore, any default by a debtor (not recoverable because of depreciation in the price of the assets used as collateral below the volume of the loan) has a relatively high impact on the equity level, and may make it difficult for the bank to fulfill the Minimum Equity Rate Requirement. To make it short, if a debtor of a bank defaults on a loan and the bank has to write off most of the loan, this will have relatively immense negative impact on the equity. Sometimes even one big debtor defaulting on the loans can wipe out most of the bank's equity and endanger its solvency. Yes, the bank business is a very risky business, unless of course the government covers all the losses the banks suffer, as happens quite often. This is also why depositors fed with rumors about a bank's situation very easily panic, and try to withdraw all their deposits.

In many cases the bank cannot fulfill its obligation to the depositors, because as has already been explained, it has extended several times more credit than it has cash in its vault. From a practical and moral point of view, it is not right that a panic among depositors caused by false rumors or conspiracy theories, should cause a bank to go bust and damage all its depositors. To prevent bank bankruptcy caused by sudden pressure of panicking depositors to withdraw their deposits, the commercial banks are forced to sell assets to generate enough cash to return the deposits to the depositors. Under pressure of immediate need for cash to repay the money to the depositors, a bank will probably have difficulty selling the assets at their real value, and so the sales will most probably involve additional losses and bring the bank another step closer to the brink of annihilation. In this situation the Central Bank assumes its role as bank of the banks, or commercial-bank rescuer, and becomes the lender of last resort to the commercial banks. To fulfill this task, the Central Bank gives the commercial banks an unlimited amount of short-term loans. These loans are called discount loans, or the discount window, and are given against collaterals of assets that the bank, while under pressure, does not want to sell under their real value, just because someone caused panic among the depositors by false rumors or conspiracy theories.

By the way, if you thought that the assets the commercial bank pledges to the central bank are tangible assets, like buildings, land or machinery, you are wrong. The commercial banks' assets are mostly the loans it has given to borrowers, and their real value is influenced by the quality of the borrower, and the interest rate he is obliged to pay.

Obviously, the Central Bank does not give such loans to the commercial banks free of charge. On the contrary, it charges the highest interest rate that exists on the money market. This interest rate automatically becomes the top interest rate that the banks will be ready to pay for deposits, since for this rate they can borrow an almost unlimited volume of money from the Central Bank at any time.

Another tool the Central Banks use to coordinate the *volume of Money in circulation* is the government securities. A proportion of the government debt securities issued by the treasury to finance its deficit is freely tradable on open markets. The Central Bank is a major player in this market, by purchasing and selling these securities. While the private dealers who are also active in the debt security market are in the business to achieve maximum profits, the Central Bank's motivation is completely different.

By selling and purchasing government securities for cash money, the Central Bank has a very significant impact on the volume of credit and as such on the volume of money in circulation. We have explained above that every additional injection of cash money into the commercial banks can be leveraged potentially as additional credit at a ratio of 1 to 9 (in the USA). If the Central Bank purchases government securities, it has to pay cash money that has to be printed for them. It is not important from whom the central bank purchased these securities, since most of this additional money paid for the government securities, will end up in the checking accounts of depositors in the commercial banks'. If leveraged, it can create additional credit that will increase the *volume of money in circulation*.

On the other hand, when the Central Bank sells government securities the opposite happens. The purchasers of the government securities pay cash money to the Central Bank for the securities, and this is subtracted from the purchaser's bank account in the commercial bank. The commercial bank now lacks this money, which was previously deposited in its vault, or was deposited in the central bank vault to meet the Minimum Reserve Rate requirement. So again, to meet the Minimum Reserve Rate requirement the commercial bank needs to borrow from the central bank, or needs to encourage potential depositors to increase their deposits. For that it needs to raise the interest rate offered to the depositors. Alternatively it can turn to other commercial banks that have available money above the minimum reserve requirement rate. The consequence of all these operations is that the interest rate on deposits and interbank loans increases and money is absorbed out of circulation.

Whether the money that the central bank has used to purchase government securities is taken from the Central Bank's vault or newly printed, is not an important issue. Probably some of the banknotes, if they are too old and dilapidated, will be burned and replaced by new bills, but burning itself does not change the volume of money in circulation. To cut a long story short, whenever the Central Bank buys treasury securities it increases the potential volume of money in the circulation, and whenever it sell the securities it decreases at volume.

Not surprisingly, this Central Bank activity directly and indirectly influences the interest rate. Directly, by influencing the interest rate paid on the deposits or for loans to other banks. Indirectly, when its activity changes the price of the government debt securities itself. How does this happen? When the Central Bank buys government securities it creates an additional demand for them, until there are not enough for the existing price and any additional purchase of the debt securities will increase their price.

You may be wondering how a rise in the price of government debt securities increases the interest rate? It is just simple mathematics. If for example government debt securities were originally issued and sold for 100 $ face value, with a repayment term of 20 years and an annual yield of 5$, the interest rate achieved on this debt security will be 5%. Let us assume that after the intervention of the Central Bank, the government debt security price has increased to 110 $. This increased debt security price does not influence the nominal interest rate, which the debt security holder is going to receive on the date of redemption. It remains annually 5 % on the face value or 5 dollars. But from the point of view of the new purchaser of the debt security, who purchased it for the price of 110 dollars, the annual interest rate on the debt security will be 4.545% since 5/110=4.545.

Not a big deal? Just think about the difference of around 45.5 cents for every 100 dollars to be paid to you every year in 20 years. Still not a big deal? Maybe not if you have debt securities of 100 $, but most of the holders of debt securities, like pension funds, insurance companies, etc. have billions of dollars' worth of them.

Government debt securities are considered by the commercial banks to be relatively the most secure investment, and at existing interest rates anybody can purchase unlimited amounts of them. So logically the commercial banks, when lending to a non-government entity, will always demand a higher interest rate from the borrower than the interest rate received from government securities. The result is that when the interest rate on government debt securities changes, all the interest rates on loans will change too.

As a consequence of the selling or purchasing government debt securities, the interest rate paid to depositors by commercial banks also changes with the change in the volume of money in bank accounts.

You have probably noticed that whenever the Central Bank purchases government debt securities, this increases their price, thereby decreasing the interest rate. But it also pours additional money into circulation, thereby decreasing the tendency of the commercial banks to borrow from other banks and-or decreasing their tendency to encourage potential depositors to make new deposits, and all this decreases the interest rate too. Thus, all these tendencies are in the same direction of increasing the *volume of money in circulation*. Obviously the opposite effect will be evident if the central bank sells government debt securities, with all the factors operating in the reverse direction.

Despite its indirect character, this convoluted system of open market operation with dual effect on the interest rate is a surprisingly effective Central Bank tool for regulation of the *volume of money in circulation*.

It should be obvious by now that the Central Bank can change relatively easily the *volume of money in circulation*. It can do so by changing the minimal reserve ratio requirement from the commercial banks, by selling or purchasing government debt securities or by changing the interest rate charged on loans of last resort given to the banks. Given that this is the case, why do we still experience economic crisis so often, with high unemployment or high Inflation and financial uncertainties?

Here we came to the big "what if?" question. What if an interest rate increase does not reduce the *volume of money in circulation* and cannot influence the tendency of prices to increase, or in other words Inflation? Or conversely, what if reducing the interest rate does not help to increase the *volume of money in circulation* when there is need to encourage the economy to grow? Can this happen? The answer is definitely YES.

At times of general prosperity entrepreneurs are over-optimistic about the future, and the bankers also have a feeling of plenty and confidence.

Bankers' decisions on whether or not to approve new loans are mainly influenced by the existing economic situation, with little account taken of the potential danger of a major shift in the economy from prosperity to deflation or in opposite. This is most common when assets, whether real estate or company shares or any other possession accepted by the commercial banks as collateral against loans, are in a process of constant price increase. As the value of the assets seems to be continuously growing, the public and the bankers tend to assume that this process will carry on forever.

Usually real estate property is accepted by the banks as very good collateral. Real estate means land and land has a tendency to become a scarce resource if located in areas with good development prospects, and its price will most probably increase. Another positive factor in real estate is its long-term stability, given by the long process needed for its production. Real estate products cannot be supplied immediately (it can take years to build a new residential project). This means that loans directed to the real estate property market create a self-supporting process of price increase in the real estate market. This price increase encourages the giving and taking of ever new loans, made possible simply by the availability of credit rather than by basic economic facts. I would not expect the price of dwellings to ever exceed a certain share of the estimated future income of purchasing households, but banks calculate the limits of the loans they offer rather from the value of the asset than from expected future cash flow.

In times of prosperity, entrepreneurs feel confident about their future income and ready to take on more and more credit. As for borrowers, they have a tendency to transfer the rational responsibility for the decision on loans to the banks. After all, banks are usually the major source of finances to facilitate investment in property, and they claim to be more professional in risk management. Is it not just natural that the banks should have the final responsibility in deciding whether a purchase is feasible or not? The trouble is that in times of prosperity as the value of assets increases, banks that base their credit policy on asset value, are naturally more inclined to become less cautious in assessing the credibility of borrowers by any other measure. So the natural tendency of the banks in times of prosperity is to increase credit, and this means that the banks become a rather pro-cycle [boom-and-bust] factor. At times of inflationary pressures, when asset prices tend to rise, the banks add momentum to this process by increasing the volume of money in circulation. This self-feeding process usually continues until it blows up, explodes like a soap bubble, and precipitates an economic crisis.

On the other hand, in times of economic uncertainty characterized by unemployment, enterprise bankruptcies and falling prices, the banks are afraid to give credit and the entrepreneurs are afraid to take on new obligations even if the interest is at the lowest possible rate. In this state of affairs no interest rate decrease can help to increase the *volume of money in circulation*.

If someone tells you, "The banks are the guardians of the economy", take it with a large pinch of salt. In reality, we can state with great certainty that commercial banks act with the market trend and not against it, and by doing so they give additional momentum to existing economic trends and so help to exaggerate economic situations. When the economy is in depression the commercial banks exacerbate the depression by squeezing credit, and when the economy is in a mania of inflationary pressures, they pour additional credit into the economy. This is another reason why we need the Central Bank, which is expected to act against the economic trends and ought to be the great anti-economic-cycle instrument, helping the government to stabilize the economy.

But sometimes even the Central Bank with all its tools cannot change economic trends. In bullish times, when the masses stampede like herds of bulls to purchase more and more new assets for growing prices without careful calculation and consideration of the possible outcome of such a trend in the markets, all the Central Bank can do is watch from the side -lines as the commercial banks pump up the bubble.

On the other hand, times when the whole population loses its feeling of economic security, and many people fear the loss of their jobs and so future income, are times when despite a low interest rate business entities prefer to deposit their available money in bank vaults or repay their loans rather than purchase ever new products. These are also times when entrepreneurs lose their confidence in the future, and their expectations for future income are reduced to a level at which they do not want to incur risk and take on credit even if the price of credit is very low. The result is a general slowdown of money circulation, which is then followed by a reduction in product circulation. As the producers receive ever fewer orders, their production capacity is laid off, and more and more workers lose their jobs and their income. This causes an additional decrease in the demand for products, and so on and on. This process is also self-perpetuating because of the closing scissors effect. The banks cannot remedy the situation in these cases even if they have enough financial resources to give additional credit. At these times, like any other entrepreneur the banks need to market their product to potential clients who are ready to take the loans and create investment opportunities able to create new economic value, out of which the borrower will repay the debts and the interest at a future date.

The re-purchase of government debt securities by the Central Bank does not always help to increase the *volume of money in circulation*. Sometimes this money is likely to remain in the banks vaults, and out of circulation, and eventually the Central Bank's policy of Monetary Easing turns out to be quite useless. All this is because the entrepreneurs and the bankers have succumbed to a gloomy, very pessimistic mood about the future economic performance of the economy. This mood is reflected in a tendency to be more cautious in their decisions and more sensitive to risks.

The conclusion must be that one of the major causes of economic crisis is a lack of confidence in future income on the part of entrepreneurs, and one major reason for Inflation and an overheated economy is people's excessive confidence in future economic performance. At times of crisis you have most likely overheard some banker or other kind of economic leader saying that "all this is about lack of confidence". Yes sometimes it is even true. Confidence is a major factor in economic processes.

How can lack of confidence cause an economic crisis? - It's a legitimate question. Just to remind you, as I said at the beginning of this book, economic crisis is the recurrent discrepancy between the volume of money and the volume of products value in circulation. What form does this discrepancy take? In the last economic crisis of 2008, the money seemed to disappear from the market and the situation called "Product comes first" took over the economic landscape. Money disappeared? How and where? Into the very same institutions that created it in the first place, the banks.

As I explained in the first chapter, at the very beginning of the book, Money can change its status to Product when it takes the form of financial assets like insurance, investments in investment funds and pension funds, long-term savings in the bank. The differences between these different forms of "Money" are differences in the degree of liquidity they possess, i.e. how fast and at what level of discount they can be converted from Product into Money.

In recent decades up to 2008, the savings of US citizens declined until they reached almost negative figures. This process gained momentum from the credit policy of the banks as explained above.

Then one day US citizens woke up and discovered that they were over indebted to such an extent that their assets could not be used for additional loans, but on the contrary, their liabilities exceeded their assets. Some even grasped that it was no longer in the power of the central bank governor, bankers or even their government to rescue them, since their assets were mortgaged not to local banks but to foreign holders of US debts.

There are indications that their mood has changed as regards their propensity for saving and consuming is concerned. The very first sign of this change is that in the last five years they have reduced their debts by about 1 trillion US dollars (it looks like this, 1,000,000,000,000). Even for the US economy, this is a substantial squeeze on the volume of money in circulation, either in its potential or in its kinetic state. This decrease in US citizens' demand for credit should not surprise us if we take into account that in the same period their real estate assets lost value to the tune of 3 trillion US dollars (and it looks like this, 3,000,000,000,000). So there is still a long way to go before US citizens will be able to feel the same level of security, they enjoyed before the outbreak of the economic crisis of 2008.

The US government and the Federal Reserve (the US Central Bank) tried its best to balance this squeeze by the antidote of monetary easing, and increased its debts by 5 trillion US dollars. (Which looks like this: 5,000,000,000,000). Yet as might be expected none of this has worked, because neither the US government, nor the Federal Reserve Bank, nor even the commercial banks, can increase the volume of products in circulation to this extend. This can be done only by the US citizens themselves. And so long as they have no faith in the US economy (and my wild guess is, it is somehow connected to the US government deficit and accumulated debt to the Chinese) they will continue to reduce their demand for credit and increase their savings.

Data source;
www.federalreserve.gov/releases/z1/Current/z1.pdf

A very different situation in which a central bank's monetary policy can become ineffective is when there is Deflation caused by the scarcity of some fundamental resource, like energy, raw material, or food production capacity but also entrepreneurship, availability of venture capital, professionally skilled work power, etc. As I have said, the scarcity of just one basic resource can be enough to create an upper limit on production capacity, and so even if a substantial part of the workforce is unemployed, this does not help much to increase the volume of money in circulation. If the production limit coincides with an increase of volume of money in circulation, the result will be both inflation and unemployment.

The scarcity of one necessary resource needed for production will restrict the whole chain of the production process of the products. It is enough for there to be a shortage of one basic resource to create a bottleneck situation preventing an increase in production.

The most obvious and recent example of this phenomenon has been sudden scarcity of oil, which a few decades ago became a major reason for inflation and the unemployment of production capacity. On a rather lesser scale, a shortage of other basic raw materials which are hard and relatively expensive to replace can cause the same effect. The result of this kind of scarcity is a stagnation of the economy combined with inflation, known as **Stagflation.** Stagflation is inflation caused by the limited capacity of an economy to increase *the volume of products in circulation* at existing price levels because of the relative scarcity of some key raw material or energy source.

I must emphasize that scarcity in a market economy does not mean that the raw material does not exist. It means simply that it is not available at a relevant price for its use. Even at times of the biggest oil crisis, oil will be available, but as the fuel price soars to new heights its use will be beyond the reach of car owners, and so it will become economically irrelevant as car fuel.

The usual solution to stagflation caused by shortage of some basic resources is the development of a new technology. Experience has shown that the very best stimulus for the technological solution of a major resource deficiency is the deficiency itself. So let us hope it will always work out that way. The stability of the natural environment as one of the resources needed to sustain the economy. Stability of the natural environment is becoming ever scarcer, and the tools to sustain environmental stability are becoming more and more costly. Thus it imposing an ever - increasing tax on the economy and reduces its growth. The best example is the air, which until recently was free of charge for everybody, and so not a Product. But lately it has become a Product with a price. Those who use air on a larger scale, like production facilities, have to pay a tax for using air - either because when designing a new product they must take the environmental impact of the product into consideration, or because they must adapt the production facility to the standards forced on them by the government and its regulators.

11. Fractional Reserve Banking, the greatest "luftgesheft" of all.

What exactly is Fractional Reserve Banking? As I explained above, the commercial banks use the money deposited in their vaults to give loans. They also have an obligation to give the depositor his money back on demand. In order to secure the stability of the commercial banks, they have to keep a certain proportion (rate) of these deposits as bank reserves in the vault of the Central Bank to comply with a minimum reserve requirement.

The Minimum Reserve Requirement imposed by central banks differs in different countries and for different types of credit. Since the rate of the Minimum Reserves Requirement is decided by the central bank, it could be a major tool of monetary policy. Yet in spite of the fact that the Central Bank supposedly has a monopoly on money creation in a country, most of the volume of money in circulation is created by the commercial banks and not by the Central Bank. This means that in the modern economy the major allocator of money is not the government or its agent the central bank, but the privately owned commercial banks.

Let us assume that the volume of money in circulation is in equilibrium with the volume of product value in circulation. The Central Bank feels it has done a great job securing smooth flow of Products and Money at full employment and without inflation pressures. Is there any further problem to solve?

Yes, there remains the question of who should create and allocate most of the volume of money in circulation: the democratically elected government and the central bank as the messenger of the government, or the commercial banks, who are in principle the "messengers" of the bank owners?

The assumption is that the commercial banks, as the main credit merchants, who are in continuous contact with the borrowers and the depositors, are the best equipped to measure and manage financial risks and so the best qualified to allocate money to the right places and for the right economic purposes in the most efficient way. As profit-oriented organizations, the commercial banks tend to lend to those who are the most likely to be able to repay their debts. According to the principles of the market economy, if finances and consequently resources are allocated to the most fit and most efficient sector of the society, they strengthen the whole economy.

Yet this arrangement begs several questions. Are the banks really the most effective tool for the allocation of money and with it resources? Is this the best way to utilize money to the economic benefit of the entire society? Are we always right to assume that the allocation of money to economically the strongest and most capable entities will necessarily create the highest benefit for the economy and the society as a whole? Is it perhaps just a system discriminating against new entrepreneurs, who very often happen to be the ones with greater potential for creating new and better economic values than the established entities?

It has to be admitted that whenever a government has taken upon itself the task of being the major allocator of the money in the economy, it has used it in very ineffective ways and often for very destructive purposes, like wars, huge white-elephant projects, or even costly social-benefit programs instituted without regard for their long-term economic consequences. Learning from this, democratic governments, encouraged by the central bank and the business community, have given up their autonomous right to allocate Money in the private sector, and left it in the hands of the banking system.

But do not forget that allocation of money is also allocation of resources. And this still leaves us with the big question, "Are the privately owned and managed banks really the right institutions to decide how to allocate most of the resources in the economy?" After all, in allocating resources, they decide who will get the chance to accumulate wealth and who will not, which fields of economic activity will get more financial resources and which less, which location gets preference in terms of investment and which does not. And all this right of decision is given to private banks, which by definition are motivated by their egoistic need to increase their own profits.

The private banks have no responsibility for the well-being of the society as a whole, or for the well-being of particular individuals. Their responsibility is to make profits for the owners of the bank. The commercial banks are not driven by some altruistic goal of redistributing the wealth according to "the needs" of the neediest, but on the contrary they help the strongest sector of the society, reckoning that the strong will be successful enough to cover their liabilities and pay some interest on top of that.

The failure of traditional banks to supply solutions for serious socio-economic problems can be vividly illustrated by the example of the women of Bangladesh. These women were the poorest of the poor, but in fact credible enough to repay the very small loans they needed to start a small enterprise of their own to rescue them from complete poverty. Yet the regular commercial banks were unwilling to accept the challenge of trying to evaluate the risks on these loans. It had to be done by an individual, the Nobel Prize laureate Professor Muhammad Yunus, who came up with the "revolutionary idea" of giving them loans in spite of all. And the idea worked! These very poor ladies of Bangladesh turned out to be much more trustworthy borrowers than some over-indebted governments and huge corporations.

In how many places in the world is there a similar need that could be solved by this system of small-scale credit, which the commercial banks are unable to provide? On the other hand, how many times have the commercial banks wasted financial resources on massive loans that just end up as un-repayable debt burdens on sovereign states, or on loans to already over-indebted exposed corporations? In many cases both the bankers and the borrowers, afraid to admit their mistake in creating mounting un-repayable debts, have a mutual interest in covering up their faults. Couldn't those resources be invested in a more useful way? Couldn't they fund other ventures that are better than creating debts to support failed governments or corporations?

If we compare the politicians and the bankers, it is clear that whereas politicians need to be regularly re-elected by the people they claim to represent, bankers, in theory are appointed by the owners of the banks. And who are the owners of the banks? Not the depositors, who have deposited their cash in the bank vaults and create most of the monetary basis for the bank's activities, but the bank's shareholders who hold most of the bank's equity. But the majority of the bank owners are small shareholders, too numerous to have any real ability to influence the bank's policy and the bank's management leadership. In practice most of the banks are controlled by minority shareholders with t a share of the bank's equity that while still small in absolute terms is sufficiently concentrated to give them real decision-making power at the annual general meetings of shareholders. This means that the equity value with the decision-making power usually represents only a very small fraction of the overall equity value, and an even smaller fraction of the total volume of deposits forming the monetary basis for the banks activity.

It seems to be wrong that the majority bank owner, which is essentially a public composed of many small share-owners, has no influence whatsoever on the appointment of the bank top management and even less on management decisions. Meanwhile the owners of the controlling shares in the bank, even though these shares represent quite a small share of the ownership structure, still have all the authority to decide on these matters. On top of this discrepancy in the ownership structure, the major monetary source making it possible for banks to operate is actually the depositors' money, while the equity of the shareholders is less than 10% of the banks' dispensable money. The banks are supposed to secure and use the deposits optimally to the benefit of the depositors. Relying on the professional skills of the bankers, the depositors gave them absolute autonomy as to whom, why and how to lend these deposits.

It is hard to explain why the managements of privately owned commercial banks, which are appointed by an anonymous body of shareholder representatives who have no direct connection either with the majority of shareholders or with the general public depositing its money in the bank, have the power to allocate money that they never earned and does not belong to the institution they head. Even the government has to be positively perceived by the majority of the public, and has to win public approval to be able to implement its policy of collecting taxes, and providing services. There is no such constraint on the banks.

Surely, if bankers are given such autonomy in a task as central to the economy as the allocation of up to 90% of financial resources in a country, they would have to be absolutely infallible not to be tempted by all the opportunities and contacts they meet in the course of their jobs. Do you believe they are more infallible than any ordinary mortals? Judging by the performance of the commercial banks in recent decades, they seem far from perfect. Here are just some of the big mistakes they have made:

Exaggerated personal rewards to the bank managers based on short-term performance, with no correlation between reward and the more important long-term performance. This kind of reward has cast an unflattering light on the warped moral judgment of not only the bankers but also the boards of directors who approved these rewards.

Another vice of the commercial financial system is the tendency to shift credit from financing investments to financing consumption. Whereas credit channeled to investments in new economic ventures and increased product production capacity is sustainable in the long run, excessive consumer credit is not. The focus of bank activities on consumer credit has encouraged unrestrained prodigal consumerism, which in itself cannot create potential economic added value in the future and so secure the loan principal and interest repayments. The practice of basing assumptions of ability to repay on the borrower's existing income and assets has led to over-extension of the liabilities of the private household, which in times of crisis, unemployment and economic uncertainty has not only caused economic misery to the credit-exposed individuals or businesses, but damaged the banks' performance too. Above all, this practice reduces the purchasing power of the society as whole at times of deflation, exactly when the opposite is most needed.

Another crucial mistake made by the banks has been the massive allocation of financial resources to purchase the sovereign debts of governments in Europe and other regions in the world that had accumulated irresponsibly high debts clearly in excess of their ability to repay. This not only brought the world financial system to the brink of collapse, but also channeled financial resources into very bad forms of utilization. These funds could have been used for infrastructure projects in less developed regions where lack of infrastructure is a major bottleneck preventing economic growth, and so every effective infrastructure project brings relatively high economic rewards. Instead the resources were used for big white-elephant projects with no economic justification, which probably enriched certain individuals but not the bank owners, and even less society as a whole.

A further error of the banks has been over-concentration on real-estate financing. This created property bubbles that eventually had to burst because residential prices were inflated beyond the point where people with average incomes could reasonably afford to purchase property. Ordinary people ended up taking on liabilities exceeding their repayment capacity.

Judging by the behavior of the banks before the 2008 economic crisis, it looks as if their policy was to discover more and more new forms of credit to allocate more and more finances just because of their practically unlimited capacity to generate more and more money and not because they created new potential of economic value. The banks have become the major contributor to all kinds of financial bubbles, and are the major cause of economic ups and downs. Because it is based on the principle of leveraging the small deposits of widely spread depositors into a big volume of credit, the commercial bank activity encourages the boom-bust cycle. The volume of bank credit grows when the economy is prosperous or bullish, and shrinks when it seems to be is in crisis or bearish. This means that banks act exactly opposite to the needs of stable economy.

The pattern of allocation of finances by the banks, as described above, runs counter not only the interests of the general public, but also to the principles of correct banking, which is supposed to support economic activities that enlarge the economic prospects of the whole society, and also secure maximum profitability for the shareholders and the depositors of the banks.

All these negative issues obviously add up to a strong case against leaving it to the bankers to be the sole decision-makers on to whom and how to allocate financial resources. Still, we need to ask whether we know of any alternative financial system that would secure a better mediation between deposits and loans, or at least do it as well as the existing banking system? The democratically chosen politically motivated government appears to be even less able to produce correct financial allocations. The focus of governments on short-term problems and short-term solutions a-priori disqualifies them.

Long-term economic problems cannot be solved by groups as short–sighted as politicians, whose survival is dependent on electorates. Since there is no alternative to the existing system, should we then leave it as it is? The answer is probably yes, but at least the obvious absurdities in the existing banking system should be checked, verified and corrected.

Ever since the economic crisis of 2008, but even earlier, public debate on finances has been concentrated on the issue of the public and particularly government deficit. Yet the real issue is not the government deficit itself. After all, the government could decide to buy back all its debts by printing more money, and if this caused upward pressures on general prices, it could increase the Minimum Reserve Rate Requirement to maintain the stability of the volume of money in circulation. By doing so it would reduce the role of the commercial banks and accordingly increase the government role as finance and resource allocator.

In fact the main problem is not how the government deficit is financed, but who is in charge of the monetary side of the economy. So the government deficit is less financial and more a political question. As we said chapters ago, the major political question is, "Who is in charge?" In this case the question is, "Who is in charge of the Money?" The government? Or the commercial banks, with the Central Bank in between? Today's system is obviously tilted towards the commercial banks. The government deficit, financed by debt securities or printed new money, is the government's only tool apart from taxation for getting a share in the process of economic resources allocation. Of course the commercial banks, their clients, the Central Bank and most of the economists, out of awareness of bad experience with government management but also out of a wish to retain their existing position in the economy, try to reduce the government's role as allocator of financial resources to the minimum.

Maybe it would not be such a bad idea to give the government a bigger role in the financial market decision-making process. After all, in a way the government represents the majority of the people. Yet the system should put the government under the same constraints as any private commercial entity. If it makes calamitous mistakes, it should be punished by annihilation, as happens to privately owned entities.

Yet the question remains: Is it right that the government should allocate most of the resources, even if under strict discipline of a well-planned expenditure, deficit and investment plan? Is there not always a risk that it will at least partly bring back a centrally managed economy, with all its faults, by the back door? If we do not want to let this happen, because of the government's flaws as a manager, some kind of alternative banking system will have to be created, which will decide on whether or not to give loans on criteria that will probably be very similar to those of the existing commercial banks, and which will aim primarily to produce maximum profit to the owners, with minimum risk.

12. Capitalism and what next?

The two main competing economic systems known as the Communist and the Capitalist systems are important, intertwined themes in this book. The Communist system derives its name from community and the communal, meaning what is or should be shared by all, while the Capitalist system takes its name from Capital, or the net value accumulating in companies and other forms of private ownership.

I am not particularly fond of either name, because I don't think either expresses the essence of the system concerned. In this book I have tried to explore the differences between them less in terms of their ideologies and more with an eye to how they function and how relatively functional they are. This is why rather than speaking of "Communism" I have preferred to use the term Centrally Managed Economic System, which highlights its practical macro-economic management system and not its ideological content. Similarly, instead of the "Capitalist Economic System" I have mostly talked about the "Market Economy", because the terms capital or capitalism refer to only one element of this economic system, which is its unprecedented drive to accumulate wealth, or in other words its propensity to concentrate possession of assets in the hands of the few. By contrast, the term "Market Economy" defines the essence of the internal instrument by which this economic system functions. I might have called it the "Free-Floating Price System", or "The price-based resource allocation system ", but both these names are unfamiliar to the reader and again identify only one aspect of the system. The Price is a major tool for allocating resources, whereas the term Market Economy correctly highlights the Market - the meeting place of the demand and the supply of the Money and the Product, the creditor and the debtor, savings and investment, and also the place where the price itself is fixed. From the perspective of more than twenty years since the collapse of the Soviet communistic economic system, looking back on the events of the 20th century, I am amazed at the fact that most of the major events of the century are uncompromising wars between these two systems: the

"Capitalist Market Economy", and the "Communist Centrally Managed Economy". Yet most of the differences between the two systems can be defined in practical economic terms.

If assessed and compared from a distance, the two systems that were so locked in conflict until the last decade of the 20th century in fact seem surprisingly close. If any difference can be identified it is more in their economic practical sides than in the substance of their basic beliefs.

If we focus on the economic aspect of the conflict, we find that the two systems essentially have the same foundation. They presuppose the capacity of humankind to govern its destiny and reject the idea of some controlling God. Both systems believe in rationality as the tool for solving political, economic and social problems. Both systems emphasize that the final goal of any political activity is to help every human individual achieve happiness by material means. Both systems believe in scientific progress as the humanity's ultimate tool for achieving this political aim.

It seems crazy that the human race teetered on the brink of self-destruction for almost half a century for the sake of small ideological differences. I want to try and get away from ideology. After all, what are ideologies but verbal structures of esoteric or supernatural half-truths, sometimes logically connected, sometimes not connected at all, which are presented dogmatically as the only and ultimate truth and are translated into political action? Unfortunately history teaches us that these half-truths, when threatened by a different kind of half-truth, or disbelief, can inspire the bloodiest conflicts humanity has ever encountered.

As it emerges from this book, the Market Economy seems to have the capacity to achieve its goal of generating wealth more effectively than the Centrally Managed economy, and what is more, the system does not limit freedom of choice on the personal and institutional level but tends to support it. Yet the "Market Economy", is also far from perfect. And here I would like to ask a provocative question, **Is the capitalistic, liberal,**

market economy secure against the total system collapse that we witnessed in the case of the Communist system in the years 1989-1992?

As I said at the beginning of this book, economic theories are needed and exist because the world's economic resources are limited, or, in the language of this book, because of the short blanket in the cold room. Of course, human beings can imagine a world where there is no limit to resources, or rather where the blanket is always big enough. This world has several names, but the most common is the Land of Eden. In many occasions in human history when people have attempted to make the land of Eden a reality on earth, such experiments have always ended in disaster, but it is worth wondering what it would be like if the experiment were ever a success. Would Eden be a world where we would really like to live? Just try to imagine a world where every wish, every desire, every request, every lust, every appeal, would be immediately fulfilled with no need to make any effort or sacrifice. Would we really be happy in such a world? Would the things we wanted and so obtained immediately have any value for us? Would such an existence have any value for us? Would life have any value? Most probably not. Yet this is the only world in which products would have no price and no value, and there would be no need for money or for economists. I wonder - is this the Utopia that human beings see as their final solution?!?

Luckily for economists, the real world is a very long way away from this utopia and still needs them. Just as it needs the bankers and politicians, who in one way or another try to their best distribute the limited existing resources and wealth (not always successfully).

If we want to define a skillful macroeconomic policy, we must recognize that it has to be worked out with account taken of the different goals and instruments appropriate to different policy time-scales. Schematically speaking, we can divide macroeconomic policy into short-term, medium-term and long-term. In any major decision on economic policy, the effects for all three time-scales must be weighed up, with an understanding that what is positive for one time scale may be problematic for another.

Major short-term economic problems usually arise at times of economic crisis. In the terms I have used in this book they may be summed up as the problem of how to create equilibrium at fully employed production capacities between the volume of money in circulation and the volume of product value in circulation.

In cases of sudden deep short-term economic crisis, the government has no option but to act without consideration for medium or long-term goals. It has to be like a firefighter, whose only concern is to put out the fire and save those trapped in it, and who rightly does not allow worries about causing damage to interfere with this priority. Once the emergency has passed the government should then act out of medium and long term considerations, with the aim of creating economic stability, as close to the full utilization of resources as possible.

The "fire-fighting" approach was adopted by the USA and Europe when the economic crisis erupted in 2008. Luckily people had learned from the catastrophic consequences of the events following the 1929 crisis, and so the US and European governments made massive interventions in the economy, pouring unprecedented trillions of US dollars into the banking system even though this ran counter to all the basic beliefs of the decision-makers.

As always, there was a medium- and long-term price to be paid for the emergency short-term fire-fighting. For example, saving the financial system involved violation of the sacred custom and norm of the market economy, indeed the moral principle of the market economy, i.e. "those who fail have to pay the price of reduction, and those who fail totally pay the price of annihilation". The financial system was bailed out, and rescued, but at the price of preserving the managers and management systems responsible for the crisis. No substantial penalty was paid by those who caused the default, and the bankers are still entrenched in their positions and fiercely wielding their influence against reform of the existing financial system.

Medium-term economic problems are of a rather different nature. The basic challenge is how to ensure continuous economic growth and the on-going process of wealth accumulation, and also a distribution of this wealth and income among the people that is equal enough to ensure decent living for all. I should stress that when I talk about the redistribution of the wealth, I mean not just between the rich and the poor in individual countries, but between the "rich" countries and the "poor" countries. In my view the main difference between the rich and poor countries is less a matter of the relative size of GDP per capita (Gross Domestic Product), which is the usual fixation of economists, than of contrasting cultures of consumption.

Many people are convinced that the gap between the rich and poor is growing, but in global perspective it is actually diminishing. Since the Second World War, and at an increasing tempo in recent decades, more and more countries have been entering the race for accelerated economic growth and adaptation to the consumerist values of the "rich" countries.

In the first years after the end of the Second World War, the only real consumer society in the world was the USA, with a population of just over 200 million. Back then US society already enjoyed most of the luxury and waste of all the advanced societies today (obviously judged by the technological standards of the time), including the most profligate phenomenon of all - the private car. This level of consumption has now become the norm and the standard for billions of people.

How many people are living this "modern" life style of consumerism in the world today? At a smart guess I would say more than 2.5 billion people out of seven. Why 2.5 billion? Well, there are about 1 billion private cars running on the roads of the globe today. The private car is the ultimate example of a product with negative cost-effectiveness that only rich people or people in countries with over-consumerism can afford to own. It is expensive and not very efficient as a means of transportation. Since most of the cars are in the economically highly developed nations, with about two people per one car in a family, this adds up to around 2.5 billion people who can afford the "modern" life-style of consumerism and waste.

This number holds up even if we estimate it by another route. The overall population of the economically highly developed nations is approximately 1 billion. Add to it the approximately 20% of the rest of the world that is rich and we are back with about 2.5 billion people. This means there are still about four billion people in line to join the club of consumer societies. Out of these, at least two billion are living in China, India and South -East Asia, countries already knocking on the door of the wealthy nations. With their annual economic growth of between 5-10% they will be through the door within a few years. China already has the biggest car market in the world. More than five hundred million South and Central American people are next in the line.

Another medium-term economic goal is the drive of market economies for continuous economic growth. Why are all the economists and consequently all the economic decision - makers so obsessed with economic growth? Is it perhaps because economic growth seems the perfect way to satisfy the human ambition to keep on advancing towards that ever receding "Land of Eden"?

Historically economic growth started about two hundred years ago, with the beginning of the industrial and technological revolutions. Meanwhile hunger and epidemics, which had been the main hazards causing recurrent demographic calamities, were broadly overcome. Yet as technology advanced and the capacity to fulfill human needs increased, it became ever clearer that human "needs" were in fact unlimited. This became the dynamo behind the continuous increasing demand for products, in turn facilitating continuous economic growth.

If you look at the data on the world economy, you will find that it just keeps on growing. Even after the economic crisis of 2008 economic growth did not stop but on the contrary accelerated. It is true that the "rich", countries have been tending to stagnate since 2008, but more and more "poor" countries have jumped on the train of high-speed economic growth, and this has more than made up for the relative sluggishness of the "rich" countries' economies.

To support this growth governments and financial institutions in the modern economies created a financial system which continuously increases the volume of money in circulation to prevent the situation that in this book we call "Product comes first". This policy inaugurates continuous economic growth. Is it possible that economic growth has only positive sides? Probably not. Yet I can't remember coming across an economic study that speaks negatively about economic growth. Why is that so? Why this universal support for economic growth? My answer is that the existing economic system depends on growth for its sustainability.

Dependence on economic growth is given by the continuous need of capital investment, whether in loans or in equities, to generate additional wealth, or what the economist call yield. If the economy stopped growing, it would stop generating additional wealth on the macroeconomic level. Some individual enterprises might still be above-average successful, but without economic growth the economy as a whole would be unable to generate additional wealth. An economy based on credit, where borrowers have to continuously repay interest, where investments need to generate additional yield on capital and also to meet continuous demand for increase of wages, simply has to grow and generate additional wealth indefinitely. Whenever the economy ceases to grow and stops creating an increased added volume of product value, the banks will have problems obtaining repayment of the loans they gave the borrowers, not to speak of the interest they charge on them. The only way the borrowers can meet their obligation to the banks is either by reducing wages or reducing their own profits. Neither of these alternatives is very feasible except in times of perceived acute economic crisis.

Add to this the problem of indebted governments when economies stagnate. If the government sincerely wants to repay these debts and the interest on them, the only alternative policy to economic growth is to cut into consumption "now". As we have already observed, forcing reductions in consumption on populations (electorates), is something that politicians are very reluctant to do.

The other reason why continuous economic growth is necessary is the inevitability of increasing productivity, for good or bad, in a competitive market economy. Raising productivity per employee increases the competitiveness of the economy and its capacity to create additional wealth, but if the labor force remains stable in numbers or even expands demographically, and the economy is stagnating, the inevitable result of increased per capita productivity is unemployment with all its negative consequences.

Since the financial system is based on expectation of generating additional wealth, if the market economy stopped growing then sooner or later this expectation would be disappointed and some kind of economic crisis would be inevitable. So one of the traps of the market economic system is its dependence on continuous economic growth.

Continuous population growth is another factor influencing the global macro-economy. Even if the population growth rate seems to be slowing down, in absolute terms it is still enormous. At the end of the Second World War the world population was about 2 billion, but today it is well over 7 billion. As we are told by experts on demography, even though in recent years the rate of population growth has dropped, over the last forty years the global population has been increasing by an additional one billion people every 12-13 years. Most of this population growth has been occurring in the poorer parts of the world.

The trend for more and more countries to enter the circle of rich, over-consuming societies, together with population growth, is putting growing pressure on the use of world resources. Is this trend sustainable? If not, depletion of world resources, including environmental stability (in fact a resource, although often not perceived as one), is inevitable. And here we have arrived at a long-term economic problem (or at least I hope it is long-term!): the problem of limited world resources and global capacity to cope with the environmental imbalances that human activity creates on the planet.

If we look for long term goals beyond those defined in the midterm, they have to relate to more than the goal of increase in material wealth. All I can see as relevant values worth sacrifices are the goals of protecting human civilization, accumulated knowledge, culture and its diversity. To this I would probably add nature too, but it seems hopeless. Given progress in the development of knowledge in scientific and technological fields such as matter, energy, mind and brain, biology, microbiology and medicine, but also social sciences, psychology and understanding of consciousness, within 30 -50 years from now humanity will be scientifically and technologically somewhere else. Humans will have skills that used to be considered the preserve of the gods. The long-term is the time it will take until this stage is reached. But there are many dangerous traps and pitfalls on the way. The main ones are the environmental trap, the population growth trap and the cultural trap.

So what are the long-term economic problems that could endanger the market economic system? The most obvious long-term economic problem to springs to mind is depletion of major economic resources. Which are the most important resources in apparent danger of depletion? Probably you would say energy or maybe some basic raw material.

A shortage of energy or other important material might well be solved technologically. And even if there is no immediate technological solution, the market economic system has tools to cope with this kind of problem, as was evident in the middle of the first decade of the new millennium. In 2006-2007 a year before the world economy collapsed, raw material prices jumped two- or three-fold. Many will remember the jump in the fuel price, but the same was true of other commodities such as most metal ores, and basic food crops. Was this the first sign of the collapse of the market economic system?

Definitely not. Even though this hike in the price of basic raw materials and energy sources may well have been one of the triggers of the 2008 economic crisis and near breakdown of the whole financial system, it was followed by an immediate squeeze on the world economy, and concurrently raw commodity prices collapsed and stabilized at a new, sustainable level. To me this is the best proof that the system of market economics did not collapse with the near implosion of the world economy, as happened less than two decades before to the centrally managed system, but on the contrary demonstrated its capacity to stabilize the world economy. Taking the crude oil barrel price as indicative, if in 2000 its price was around 20 US Dollars per barrel, before the crisis it rose to almost 140 US Dollars per barrel, but then collapsed with the crisis to 30 US Dollars per barrel. Now five years after the outbreak of the crisis it is around 100 US Dollars per barrel, which shows an upward trend but is still a sustainable price level. Not surprisingly all the other raw materials have followed the same pattern.

As regards the foreseeable future, new technologies likely to be introduced in the coming decades will provide solutions to the problem of creating supplementary sources for basic raw materials and energy. The solution may not always be "just in time", and so from time to time the economy will have to cope with exaggeratedly high resource prices, but these price increases will probably just accelerate initiatives to find alternative solutions.

All the same, there is still one major economic resource for which science and technology appears unable to find a solution without the cooperation of politically motivated governments. This resource is the environmental sustainability of the global eco-system.

Here we come to the primary long-term problem of the world economy: world environmental stability. If we believe that the depletion of the world's resources is an inevitable process (and this is a question of faith and not conclusively based on evidence), we must believe that the world environment as a major resource is also limited. Yet any policy of creating ecological sustainability demands substantial revolutionary sacrifices of the "modern human life style", and the liberal democratic political system does not appear to have the tools for the introduction of such a policy.

There is a prevailing belief that natural and economic systems have an inner self-correcting regulator that will always in mysterious ways bring the whole system back to a new balance and equilibrium point after a crisis. In fact, this same belief was behind a number of catastrophic economic policy decisions in the past, most notably the series of horrendous errors made by the US president, government and Federal Reserve governor in 1929, when the Great Economic Crisis first broke. These errors ensured that the world economy remained in turmoil for the next 60 years. Only with the collapse of the USSR did the effects of this crisis and its persisting negative impact on a large part of the world's population diminish.

Less than 20 years after the collapse of the communist system, the world economy found itself in a new crisis. And once again, behind the justification for the financial institutions to continue with a policy obviously tending to upset the equilibrium of the financial system, we find the same belief in an automatically self-correcting system.

If like me you believe in the fable of the short blanket, but do not believe in the other fable of the possibility of creating Eden here on Earth, you will have to agree that these trends of over exploiting world resources will have to be stopped one day, and better sooner than later.

As I said above, the financial system was recently saved by the intervention of governments, which are external to it. If crisis overtakes the world environmental system, will governments be able to save it in the same way? Does the existing decision-making system based on democratic principles have the internal strength to prevent the collapse of the world into environmental imbalances?

We could cite many examples of the dysfunction of the market economy, but the major prospective failure of the market economy is in coping with the long-term problem of environmental ecological functionality. Who can say which additional billion of people, or which increase in consumption, may tip the world environment right off balance and bring the world economy to a breaking point and a crisis on a scale never experienced before?

I recently found a wonderful description of this reality in an article in "Nature, international weekly journal of science" published on 7.8.2012

http://www.nature.com/nature/journal/v486/n7401/full/nature11018.html

It is now well documented that biological systems on many scales can shift rapidly from an existing state to a radically different state. Biological 'states' are neither steady nor in equilibrium; rather, they are characterized by a defined range of deviations from a mean condition over a prescribed period of time. The shift from one state to another can be caused by either a 'threshold' or 'sledgehammer' effect. State shifts resulting from threshold effects can be difficult to anticipate because the critical threshold is reached as incremental changes accumulate and the threshold value generally is not known in advance. By contrast, a state shift caused by a sledgehammer effect—for example the clearing of a forest using a bulldozer— comes as no surprise. In both cases, the state shift is relatively abrupt and leads to new mean conditions outside the range of fluctuation evident in the previous state. Threshold-induced state shifts, or critical transitions, can result from 'fold bifurcations' and can show hysteresis. The net effect is that once a critical transition occurs, it is extremely difficult or even impossible for the system to return to its previous state. Critical transitions can also result from more complex bifurcations, which have a different character from fold bifurcations but which also lead to irreversible changes.

Since the beginning of the seventies, scientific data have indicated that human beings are living beyond the carrying capacity of planet Earth and this cannot continue indefinitely.

Yet among economists, bankers and politicians it is still the generally accepted wisdom that a healthy economy is a growing economy, and many of them believe that over-consumption is the essential fuel for healthy economic growth. The growing economy needs a growing demand, and growing demand needs growing consumption. This chained logic has been behind the policy of governments when they have done everything in their power to pump new energy into private consumption at times of economic crisis. This idea is especially dominant in US economic policy, (the best example is the tax rebate given by the US government to every US citizen when the crisis of 2008 was at its height).

But this is a very short-term solution with rather negative long-term effects. In the long-run it will damage the US economy and increase its trade deficit problem, which will ultimately have to be faced and tackled one way or another.

Can we imagine an economic system that would make long-term global environmental sustainability a major goal? What kind of economic and political system would such a goal require? Most probably today's system of sovereign countries, each of them acting egoistically, is not very helpful when it comes to solving the problem of world environmental sustainability.

If a government made world environmental sustainability its major goal, what economic and political steps would it have to take?

Is every kind of economic growth ecologically damaging? Definitely not! Growth that does not demand world resources, energy and raw materials is not damaging in this way. Examples include the business of recycling or producing alternatives to basic raw materials like carbon - and silicon-based nanotechnology materials that can substitute for metal materials, biotechnological processing methods that are alternative to conventional agriculture productions, alternative energies that do not have ecological footprints like wind energy, solar energy, fusion atomic energies, geothermal energies, etc. Most of these new technologies are not yet available, and so the economic growth should be a matter of investing in the development of these technologies but definitively not of subsidizing 80% of the consumer prices as happened with solar energy panel development in Europe. Economically and also ecologically these products were counter-productive and did not meet expectations, while scientists working on laboratory prototypes with as yet uncertain feasibility outcomes still cannot access funding for the further development of their ideas.

Even in food production, the emphasis should be on food produced using biological processes that have a positive ecological footprint. A good example is support of food production from vegetation consuming CO_2 out of the atmosphere, and not from livestock with its huge negative impact on the world environment. Agriculture is one of the ecologically most devastating of human economic activities. It occupies most cultivable land, leaving only marginal land (mountains, uninhabitable regions) to the natural world.

Many see agrarian activity not only as a food producing activity, but as part of the cultural heritage of their countries, and even cultivated fields as the countryside's natural state. Yet if land used for agricultural production were integrated into natural systems, something more like a genuine natural state would return.

The other long term economic issue is how to achieve more even distribution of world income and wealth. Here the challenge is mainly for the rich highly developed countries to give up some of their wealth in a smart way, so as to increase wealth distribution all around the world. They should not be doing it out of altruism but to safeguard their own existence. The economic policy of environmental sustainability is a luxury that only rich people can afford.

One of the main reasons for the continuous trend of world ecological devastation is global population growth. It is evident that the population growth is occurring mainly in poor countries without a general education system, and often with cultures denying education to women. Increased income and modern education would seem to be a precondition for the reduction of birth rates. No environmental consciousness will develop in societies in which too many people are hungry and struggling for their very survival. Without environmental consciousness, it will be impossible to halt the trend of ecological devastation.

Added value Equals the price for which a product is sold to the next stage in the production process, minus the cumulative cost of all the components needed to create the product in the previous stages of the production chain. It is created in each step of the production process. Eventually it equals the total net income generated during the whole production and sale process.

Bank notes Cash money in the form of paper.

Central Bank The central bank's main task is to create trust in Money. The central bank has to make people believe that the scarcity of money is exactly as needed to enable the volume of product value to circulate without obstructions at full employment, and neither more nor less.

Commercial bank Institution for depositing and borrowing Money.

Credit Loan Mortgage, postponed payments.

Currency Devaluation Process of the value depreciation of one currency against other currency.

Deflation Tendency to decrease in production caused by the tendency of the total *volume of the Value of products in circulation* to be higher than the total *volume of money in circulation.*

Equilibrium Scarcity of Money State when the volume of Money is in equilibrium with the volume of Product value in circulation.

Equity (Share capital) The value that company owners have invested in any legal entity, plus all the retained earnings accumulated by the entity during its existence, minus the dividend paid to the owners, and losses. In other words the current market value of all the company assets minus the total value of all its liabilities, except the shareholders' equity.

Government An institution that initiates laws and has power to enforce them. The duty of the government is to punish those who violate the law.

Government debt securities Government financial obligations to be repaid within an exactly specified time period, issued by the treasury to finance the government deficit.

Government Deficit The difference between the products/services provided to the population by the government and the taxes collected by the government.

Inflation General price increase which usually occurs when the *volume of the value of products in circulation* is lower than the *volume of money in circulation*

Interest rate The price of the loans the debtor is paying to the lender for an exactly specified period of time.

Loan Money borrowed today with a promise of repayment.

Minimum Reserve Requirement Percentage of total deposits the commercial banks have to keep as reserve in cash, out of the total volume of deposits.

Money A tool to give value to Products. Money can be easily transferred from one owner to another, and from immediate usage to postponed usage.

Money ready for circulation Cash in the wallet or deposited in the current bank account.

Product Everything purchasable for Money, whether merchandise or services, tangible and intangible assets, movable and immovable assets, real estates and dwellings. Products can be also financial assets like insurances, investments in investment funds, pension funds.

Stagflation General price increase combined with tendency to decrease in production, caused by scarcity of a basic raw material

Trade deficit Volume of product purchase exceeding the local product production balanced by import from other country.

Trade surplus Volume of product production exceeding the local product purchase, balanced by export to other country.

Value of money The actual purchasing power or the real value of money when exchanged for a Product.

Velocity The number of times money changes ownership over a certain period of time, or in other words the rate at which money is exchanged from one transaction to another.

Volume of money The amount of cash in your wallet or deposited in the bank account, available for immediate use.

Volume of money in circulation Equal to the volume of product value in circulation [is the exact counterpart when exchanged against the product.

Volume of product value in circulation Equal to the total volume of money in circulation. By definition there is no product that does not have value in the form of price expressed in units of money. The result is that the value of the "volume of product in circulation" is always expressed exactly as the same volume of money.

Wealth Product and/or Money accumulated in its potential state.

The author was born and brought up in a "Communist" country and emigrated as an adult to the "West", where he worked as an economic advisor in government, and was then active as a successful private entrepreneur, investment fund manager, and economic and financial advisor to many different sized companies operating in different fields of business activity. In the book the author explains in a simple and easily understandable way how the Economy works and is influenced by major economic players on an imaginary island, the economic tools they operate with, the systems of governance they use and how they cover up their failures. He vividly shares his lifelong experiences, spiced with humor and even sarcasm but, without compromising his professional explanations of today's major world economic problems.

The basic aim of this book is to explain two dimensions of economics. The first concerns the separate worlds of Money and Product, as they circulate continuously in opposite directions. The second concerns the dilemma of how to cope with the problem presented in the metaphor **"Economics is the science of a short blanket in a cold room: if you cover your feet your shoulders will be cold and if you cover your shoulders your feet will be cold".**

To make the book accessible to all, it is purposely written without use of any math, graphs, tables or academic footnotes. Though written with the lay reader in mind, it is an argumentative book, and contains original thoughts about economics and government functionality.